# PEACE IS POWER

A Course in Shifting Reality
Through Science and Spirituality

MICHELLE PAISLEY REED

Copyright © 2017 by Michelle Paisley Reed
All Rights Reserved.
No part of this book may be reproduced, stored in retrieval systems, or transmitted by any means, electronic, mechanical, photocopying, recorded or otherwise without written permission from the author.
Acme & Cambria fonts used with permission from Microsoft.

Published by TCK Publishing

www.TCKPublishing.com

Get discounts and special deals on our best selling books at

www.tckpublishing.com/bookdeals

Sign up for Michelle's free newsletter at

www.WeAreThePowerOf10.com

# PEACE IS POWER

To my daughters, V and O, the other pieces of my heart. They teach me every day more about how to love properly and unconditionally. They are the embodiment of courage and hope and strength, and together, they represent the beauty of evolution into new generations of powerful young women.

And when someone is your twin flame soul mate, you don't forget to thank him! I am grateful for every day I get to wake up next to my most amazing husband, Jodah—love of my life, partner in all things regarding The Power of 10. His "front row seat" access to their teachings has enriched both of our lives without measure.

Shout out to my sister, Nicole. Grateful you always have my back, no matter what!

My family is my golden treasure.

# Contents

INTRODUCTION ........................................................... IX

CHAPTER 1  *STRESS* ..................................................... 1

CHAPTER 2  *CELEBRATIONS* ...................................... 5

CHAPTER 3  *MAGNIFICATION* ................................. 15

CHAPTER 4  *PEACE ON YOUR PLANET* ................. 19

CHAPTER 5  *BREAKING DOWN WALLS* ................. 25

CHAPTER 6  *HOLDING SPACE FOR ONE ANOTHER* ............... 31

CHAPTER 7  *PEACE* ................................................... 33

CHAPTER 8  *ABUNDANCE FOR ALL* ...................... 37

CHAPTER 9  *IMPEDIMENTS* ..................................... 41

CHAPTER 10  *SOAKING IT ALL IN* ........................... 45

STEP BEYOND ............................................................ 49

THE BOOK OF EUDICINE ......................................... 147

THE BOOK OF MYAGANA ....................................... 167

THE BOOK OF PILARA ............................................. 183

THE BOOK OF THERAS ............................................ 197

| | |
|---|---|
| THE BOOK OF LAVINIA | 213 |
| ABOUT THE AUTHOR | 231 |
| OTHER BOOKS BY MICHELLE PAISLEY REED | 233 |
| BOOK DISCOUNTS AND SPECIAL DEALS | 235 |

# Introduction

There is a space beyond, a glorious place in fact, where we belong.

The Power of 10 is a collective of spirits who chose to leave their bodies behind and move beyond the life-and-death cycle into higher dimensions of peace, Love, and a word that is beyond your "bliss."

By now, you've heard of us. By now, you are living many of the Truths we set out for you in the first book, *Manifesting Miracles and Money: How to Achieve Peace, Purpose, and Plenty Without Getting in Your Own Way*. If you are not, you may need to give that first book another read through. Use the tools. Allow them to become a part of your daily existence, so that you may reach the level of frequency where you can hear these new words—where you may move up your vibration to new heights that no longer give your denser body unpleasant sensations. Even your body vehicle has perhaps given up the fight to become conscious and is re-creating at a cellular level.

It is our hope that you live a vibrant life while you are still here. It is our greatest pleasure to see you thrive, to grow in excitement about the adventure you chose in your entry-level existence. We love seeing you succeed, and success means different things to different souls, yes?

You see, we point to a place beyond the life-and-death cycle, a space where we reside, where we know of no pain, as we no longer choose to have a bodily existence. It is a dense one, yes? But it is also full of beauty, full of sensual touch and visual stimulation.

Beyond the bodily existence, you still have your senses; they are just more alive. They are set free, like a lion from a cage. They are on fire all the time, engaging your higher Self to new heights because they aren't held back by thought or doubt. There is no such thing as doubt where we reside.

And so, in this first chapter of our second book together, we would like you to play with setting your senses free. Begin by engaging them fully. As you go through your day today, start with sight. *See* everything around you with new eyes. Perhaps visualize a dial that you turn to the "up" position and see with greater clarity of vision.

If you do not have your sight, engage your inner vision. Do this anyway. Fully engage your inner and outer vision to experience your day fully. Perhaps do this for several days if it is enjoyable to you. And then move on to hearing, touching, tasting. Wait a day in between, just for fun.

By the end of the week, your senses should be at new levels where you are engaging with your world in ways you never imagined. You were born with these senses, and as a baby, you were enthralled with them. It is thrilling to go from being in Spirit to being in a body, each and every time you do it. So learn to enjoy the body. Acknowledge your body, and it will not keep trying to get your attention with the pain paradigm.

Notice when your body is hungry, and feed it higher-vibrational foods that come from the earth, not from a factory. Don't ignore your body. If your child was hungry, you wouldn't ignore its cries. Why would you do that to your poor body?

In the same way, when your body is tired, allow it to rest. Stop making excuses for why you can't do this. Your excuses are the blocks that get in the way of your highest good. When the body is tired, rest. If someone at your job says no to this, it's time to find a new space where your highest good is honored and supported.

The body needs recharging like a battery. When you get to the space where we are—a space beyond rest, where peace is ever present—you won't have to lie down. When you push yourself to do more, be more, have more, you are putting a closer expiration date on your present body. And that is not what we are suggesting you do.

You came into this present existence because you wanted to. Don't forget that. When you leave, it is indeed possible to move beyond into higher dimensions, where you no longer need suffering to learn. Believing it is possible is enough. For now, take the contrast that shows up, and learn the lessons your soul wished into existence. However, don't participate in the drama or bring it to you. Enough will come to you on its own, based on your presence within this current societal kingdom.

And yet, as you rise, less and less of the negative participation shall affect you. Instead, it will run through you like a stream. As you are living the words of our first book, together you are rising up, yes? It feels so good, and as it feels good, you shall know more GOOD. It just keeps getting better and better.

That is a new mantra for you. "It just keeps getting better and better." Say it upon waking, and gradually, you will find you're at new levels of happy. And moving beyond into new levels of happy is what this book is all about.

[**Please note:** I have chosen to capitalize words such as *Love*, *Truth*, *Spirit*, etc., throughout this book where appropriate to reflect their higher meanings. Also, please have a journal or notebook handy for the lessons, as many of them have opportunities for written reflection.]

# Chapter 1

## *Stress*

Stress is not accepting where you or others are on the journey.

If you have practiced "unzipping" your body—and we hope you have and now *see* with new eyes that you are indeed the Spirit driving around the body vehicle—we would like for you now to *build* upon this new vision, and see that the *others* around you are also driving around their bodies in the same fashion.

Unzip the bodies of those around you, and you will see the same Spirit that inhabits you *also* inhabits them.

So you see, *the stresses you feel are the unhealed parts of you that are projected in another.* Everyone around you mirrors your soul, you see. If you pretend to unzip them, you see clearly now that *they* are indeed *you*, just housed in a different form that they chose in between lifetimes. It's just like choosing a new car when you tire of the old one. Some choose to run theirs into the ground before they purchase a new one, others buy or lease one every few years, some only buy used, others only want brand new. It is only a car. It is not you.

And yet, you often judge others by their "car." Who is inside?

In the same way, when you see another, ask yourself, "Who is inside?" If another is irking you, ask yourself why you are so irked by another's chosen path? Are there changes in yourself you have not made, and seeing the other person "stuck" is easier than addressing your own hurdles?

It's all just resistance to change, which is enormously funny to us, because you can no more stop change than your Earth can stop revolving.

And when you stop allowing another's journey to impede your progress, you vibrate much higher—your revolutions go quicker, you see, and as you "spin" you'll either attract or repel whatever it is you desire!

That's how it works, you see. There are 7 billion people currently inhabiting your planet, and more souls who visit often from the way station in much lighter forms that do not require food or shelter. If your vibration repels another, it is not a "bad" thing, as you deem it. It simply means they are no longer on the same frequency and are moving along a different chosen path. Perhaps you were on the same "path" at one moment in time, but if you hold on too tightly to this person or experience that no longer feels "good," it is like holding on to a rope in a fast-moving river. Eventually, something's going to give—and once you let go of the rope, you'll find yourself traversing the river with great speed and momentum toward the people and experiences you *do* now want.

In fact, raise your vibration incrementally each day, using the tools we have taught you—more in this book—and soon, you will find others matching you *so* well that they will GIFT you the exact things and experiences you want. You will also find yourself giving to others in a greater capacity, and so in this way, you benefit and manifest for each other. And *you will find yourself attracting things and experiences you did not even know you wanted.* The greater version of You will begin to take the lead, and your higher vibration will gain momentum to lift you daily. You will eventually no longer need any tools at all but will live in constant harmony with all that is.

And yet, you can stop the flow at any time by sticking your feet in the ground and creating a story about the person who is getting in your way. It is YOU who get in your way. How do you stop, you ask? *By repeating the story of the greater Truth of who you are.* Get *so* good at telling yourself that you are a creator, that you are Divine Truth in action, that you are constantly vibrating higher and higher, and attracting all people, and situations, and energies you need to do all the things you came here to do this time around.

And no, you don't *need* to get it all done in this one little lifetime.

Affirm that you know you have experienced countless, colorful lifetimes, and your soul is multi-faceted. *Affirm* that you see your soul reflected in another's eyes, that you ALL—*all humans, all animals*—share one great Spirit, and you will know that you can *graduate* from this existence into another level, where you will not learn the "hard" way anymore.

## 4 PEACE IS POWER

As you rise, you may notice others who are still learning the hard way, but it is not for you to point this out. Simply be in their presence as it pleases you, and if they are attracted to your higher vibe, you both will rise higher. If you feel them bringing you down, perhaps choose to separate for a while until they catch up, or until they choose another who matches their lower frequencies and who isn't such a "threat" to their ego.

You choose to be drawn magnetically toward those who make your heart beat a little faster, who make you smile, who sit with you in your pain, and who demonstrate purity of Love. In that purity, you will know peace. And in that peace, you may share it with others.

## Chapter 2

## *Celebrations*

All of life is a big celebration, yes? Do you not feel this? What if you awoke each day with a feeling of celebration in your heart—as if confetti were about to drop from the ceiling—and it's as if you "won" something?

Because, in Truth, every day you inhabit a body—no matter what condition that body is in—is a cause for celebration! Do you remember how you brought forth this existence from *nothing*? While still in Spirit, you were drifting in bliss, Love, and pure connection, when you decided to come forth and create a body—to create something from nothing, to think your way into being via pure intention. You wished to CREATE, and so because you are one with all creation, you brought thought into form. You took the formless substance which is the Truth of you and every soul around you, and you took measured steps into be-ing.

And, well, here you are. Don't you believe you should celebrate?

Each night you rest, you recharge your body vehicle like an electric car. You plug in your "batteries" for the night, plug into Divine Source energy as you sleep, and you wake renewed and refreshed. *Grateful.*

Each and every day is a do-over. We've said this before, but until you LIVE what you LEARN, we will keep repeating ourselves. Each day is a do-over. What will you do with it?

And now, you are here reading this book and the one before it because you are feeling a sort of restlessness, yes? It's a feeling of completion as you start to live the tools, as you live a path, a journey, which is authentic, real, and beautiful. You notice the beauty around you, and you know how to both be present and, at the same time, to lift your vibration and amplify it to new levels. You know this.

*And so this feeling of completion, it is real.* It's as if you are at the end of a school year, and the book work is done, the tests are taken, the essays are written, and you and your teacher and classmates are just playing. You all are going to swim parties and playing outdoor games on the lawn, and perhaps taking trips to the waterslides! You are all so happy that your lessons are complete, and you feel a sense of accomplishment—you did it! You made it through the "hard" parts and have gained new knowledge and wisdom that you may build upon in the next "grade" level up.

And for now, you are fulfilled. For now, you are so proud of yourself and those who've shared your journey—yes, even the "difficult" souls who bumped up against you and taught you how to learn through contrast. You even appreciate those who tried to drag you down into their drama, and who instead, *you* brought into your extended positive aura; and those who chose to sink deeper into their perceived pain and misery, well, you love them, also. It is their choice to move into their pain rather than to learn and rise above it, and someday, they may choose differently, but for now you've demonstrated by example, and it feels good.

Do you want to throw your graduation hat in the air?

What does that symbol represent? Freedom? Because in Truth you *are* freedom. And now you realize this, but some of you go back to what you were doing that you don't really want to do.

Why?

Did someone else tell you to? What does society, your community, your family, your world expect of you? And does it really matter?

What matters?

YOU matter! You see, as we stated at the beginning of this discussion, you matter because you created yourself from formless thought, from collective Spirit, into directed matter. You *all* did this—not some man in the sky. You are made of Spirit. You are made of LOVE. Does that not resonate? If you still wish to give your power over to another, then by all means, give this book to someone else. And yet, if something deep inside you stirs when you understand that in each given moment you are creating yourself, if you understand and *know* that your cells are constantly recreating themselves, and what a miracle that is, then you know the miracle is in the moment. You can create something out of nothing, for you created your very self in this incarnation—AND, in many, many incarnations before this one! You've lived out a *whole* lot of lives—don't you feel this? You've done it the "hard" way, learning through suffering, and yet you are now in this *new* place, where you may affirm that you learn through FAITH and *not* suffering, and as your comfort level grows with this new space of presence, and as there is no feeling whatsoever of emptiness, you will manifest some more for you and others around you, simply because it is FUN! You "get" that this life thing is a game, and you have been taking it very, very seriously, when all along, you entered into it with a lightness of being, knowing that in the end, you would always return to Spirit, and that Spirit is all there is anyway.

## MANIFESTATIONS

We would like to discuss with you some tools, all of which you might have heard about before, but put in this way might be the spark that gets the objects and opportunities you long for to ignite and take form.

We would like for you, then, to focus only on what truly *matters*. You see, because then you are bringing forth into matter, into this world, those things and experiences that are most meaningful. Take some time to consider why you want what you want. What are the feelings that would come of this?

After a period of consideration, we would like to teach you about three "magic" words, all of which happen to begin with the letter "I." This will make it easier for you to remember, yes?

## IMAGINATION

Every single soul was given this gift upon birth. Imagination is the creative force of Spirit, and we'd like to remind you that you are *all* creators. You wanted to "help out" and expand the Universe by lending your contributions, and so—especially when you were a young child—your mind created all sorts of innovative ideas that a bunch of well-intentioned adults promptly squashed as being too fantastical.

And so, you might have learned at a young age not to trust those images in your mind, the pictures formed by another important "I" word, intuition.

We want you to trust those internal, inner images once more. We want you to daydream, a LOT! When you did this naturally as a child, you may have been chastised for being distracted. We'd like to teach you that this is the *opposite* of what you were doing. You were tapping directly into Divine wisdom, and the *good* news is, you can do this again as an adult.

When you are relaxed, when you are meditating or on a vacation or on a walk—whatever it is you do to clear your mind—and you see your mind wandering, where does it wander *to*? Beyond any worries, song lyrics, or dramas, what surfaces?

## INSPIRATION

What surfaces after such introspection is inspiration. The ideas you receive in quiet moments of allowance are your keys to what appear to be miracles to you. You see miracles as things that happen rarely, when, in fact, they could happen daily—even more often—if you were in a constant state of receptivity.

*What would happen if you allowed yourself to daydream daily?* Arguments about how it would disrupt your responsibilities don't belong here. If you truly want to be a constant creator, you have to learn to stop blocking your daydreaming capacities.

When doubts or fears surface, simply say hello to them, and brush them aside. It is simply a part of your human process to acknowledge fears, and when you get to the space where we reside, your fears will become nonexistent.

Try this: allow any and all fears to have a voice. What are they saying to you? *You're a fool? A failure? Others will mock and judge you? You will starve?*

Don't write those down; that would be giving them too much energy. You are far more powerful than your fears. You already realize this, or you wouldn't be reading this book right now! But do take some time to let your fears spout off their "list" of worries and anxieties until they run out of steam.

The absolute worst thing that could ever happen to you while still in bodily form is to lose your bodily form, yes? To die, in any way, shape, or form.

And yet, you have *all* died many, many, many times! You have shed your body more times than you can count, and your soul has survived all of those experiences. Your soul never, ever dies. Love never, ever dies. And so you, too, never ever die.

Now that *that* is behind you, daydream some more, and allow your inspiration to have a voice. *What does it say to you, now that you have no fears stopping it?*

## INTENTION

Once your energy has lifted, and you are feeling inspired, it is time to ignite your intention. Intention is simply putting your imagination and inspiration into action.

When the thoughts in your mind turn into images, and your vibration is lifted due to inspiration, your dreams now become an actual THING. Write down what it is you intend to do, and you will make it more concrete! Say it out loud. Check in with how it feels. Does your heart pound a little harder from excitement? If yes, then you're on the right track.

If your heart is pounding, and it feels like fear, go back to the last step, and face your fears until they go away. Breathe life into your inspiration until it feels *good*, then picture it some more. MAKE IT MATTER.

## INNOVATION

You see, all of innovation is simply imagination + inspiration + intention. Yes, another "I" word. Isn't that interesting? Traditionally, you've seen the "I" as ego, and many see the ego as "evil." And yet, without the ego on this planet, who would you be? The ego is simply the individualized unit of Spirit, sent here by YOU to create and expand. And evil is "live" spelled backward. So perhaps, instead of calling yourself a bad word just because you are doing what you came here to do, what if you embraced LIVING and affirmed that as long as you are alive, you might as well innovate?

When you are an innovator, there are *sure* to be others who will mock you. They will vibrationally congregate, commiserate, and bring each other down the ladder of emotions. And yet, there will be many more who will embrace and *celebrate* your innovative ideas, for it is those same ideas that will benefit humanity as a whole. It is those same innovations that, when engaged, will bring the Light from within you to the outside as well.

Congregate with and support the innovators in your world, and you will keep growing and gathering momentum to higher and higher levels of being. As you do so, you will come into contact with people, things, and experiences you did not know you wanted, except perhaps at a soul level.

We give as an example Michelle's recent manifestations.

She was getting her hair done by a friend who mentioned she was getting a recreational vehicle (RV) for her fiancé for his birthday. As they discussed the gift, Michelle's imagination took flight, and she was picturing herself and her family travelling in this way, and she had the inspiration that perhaps this might be a good way to travel to Power of 10 events. She had thoughts of eating healthy foods while on the road, and parking the RV beside lakes and oceans, where she longed to live. Images of drinking coffee in the morning—or wine in the evening—while looking at the water, started to make her very, very happy.

When she got home, she set the intention to learn more about RVs, and right away, she saw a television program that she might have ignored otherwise. It was called *Going RV*, and she watched it all night long.

When Michelle went to sleep that night, she had vivid dreams of driving the RV to new places, and she woke up feeling FREE!

On her way to see a client, she said a meditation/prayer out loud in the car that if she were to own an RV, she would surrender this want completely and allow it to "land in her lap."

And because she was not thinking how she "needed" an RV, because she had lifted her vibration to a new level of being that was a match to her desire, this frequency brought it to her.

She mentioned the RV to the client, who stated that his daughter wanted to donate her RV to a good cause, and he believed we were a very good cause.

That week, Michelle met with the client and his daughter, and they joyously gave it to Michelle and Jodah, who celebrated over dinner that evening!

Now they have a BIG reminder parked out in front of their driveway of how powerful manifestations can be, and of how quickly they can move into matter once you attain the correct frequency.

Now that Michelle was feeling confident about her abilities to manifest as a conscious creator, she woke up one morning to an intuitive feeling that she should look online at a shopping site called "Craigslist" for her dream hot tub. She had been shopping for one that was currently out of her budget, but she knew exactly which one would fit her deck.

And so, when she scrolled down and saw this very same hot tub that had only been used once, at a fraction of the cost, which was in her budget, she took inspired action and called right away. The seller told her it had been sold, but he would keep her in mind if the deal fell through.

Michelle told the man she was driving toward their half-way meeting point with the exact amount of cash in hand, and that she would be overjoyed at relaxing in the hot tub!

She went to lunch with a friend near the meeting point and kept imagining herself enjoying the warmth of the hot tub. Please note: she did not let her energy drop by becoming discouraged in the least. Instead, because she had allowed herself to imagine the exact model of hot tub and saw it where she wanted it, and because she already knew how it would make her feel, it *had* to come to her.

The woman who was going to purchase the hot tub never showed up. And so, Michelle was able to meet the seller at the agreed upon location for the sale.

## Chapter 3

## *Magnification*

We are coming to you now because you are all at the leading edge of transformation. You understand that you are all one, yes? There are no boundaries, no separation. You realize the power of your thoughts and the power of the word to create something from nothing—to magnetize your desires, yes? You know you came here, to this denser dimension, to test your skills at this, to create, to go on adventures, to rediscover the beauty of your world, to focus on the good and multiply it tenfold.

When you are on a roll with your manifestations, doesn't it feel *good*? Are you allowing the feelings of your manifestation to wash over you rather than *trying* (not a good word) to check off the next thing on your list?

It's important—essential, actually—to relish the good feelings of your manifestations as they happen. That is why you wanted them to begin with, yes? Perhaps you wanted the car to feel sporty and free. And now you have it. You are driving it around, feeling all free and sporty and happy and carefree! Relish those feelings! And as they start to die down, and they will, remind yourself of those early feelings of how it *felt* to manifest this new, fun thing.

Perhaps you wanted the new job, and you got it. Maybe it was a new house, and now you're living there! You've been on vacation, several times, and you have zero debt, and you're doing exactly what you came here to do. You are LIVING out your dream—which is in actuality what you set out to do between lives. Others are inspired by your example, by your radiance that shines from within, and they are living out their *own* dreams and desires.

Others feel lifted just by being in your presence. And it is enough. In fact, it is everything.

Now what?

Many of you will arrive here, to this new level of being and existing and creating, and wonder what your next step is. We get this question often in Michelle and Jodah's gatherings.

And yet, if you are not here, we'd like to encourage you to re-read our last book until you are *here*.

HERE is a place of near instant gratification, where there are no limiting thoughts or beliefs left in your brain, and you are in a constant state of appreciation. You no longer need to "do" affirmations, as your mind *thinks* in affirmation. You understand at a deeper level that you, along with everyone else in your dimension, live in a positive Universe that only wants the best for

## CHAPTER 3 - MAGNIFICATION

you. *You* want the best for you. And since "you" are the same Spirit that inhabits every other soul, "you" want the best for all others as well.

Do you want to magnify your manifesting abilities even further? Learn to give it away.

Give WHAT away, you might ask?

Whatever it is you'd like to receive, give it away first, without any expectation. It works like a boomerang out into the Universe. If you give 1% of your income to another, you will produce 1% from another source. For example, if you earn $100 in a week and you give away $1, you will get back $1 from someone else.

When you create a "void" and surrender the energy "backward," it must be filled. It is a fact. Some would call it a "law," but we try to avoid that word because it holds a somewhat negative connotation for many. This isn't a rule, but just the way things work.

When you give away your money, you create a mindset that there is plenty to go around, and so it comes back to you in turn, you see. Your money is simply an example—one example—of the manifestation of freedom. It is a symbol. And as such, if you give in generosity, it will be fulfilled. *It must.*

Taking this one step further: If you give away 10% of your earnings, you will not only pull in 10% more but 10 times 10! THIS is the power of 10—multiplied! And so, using the same example, if you earn $100 in a week and you give away $10, you will receive $1,000! Just don't expect it from the same source, you see. Allow it to come from wherever.

## EVERYTHING IN YOUR UNIVERSE WORKS IN ONES AND ZEROS

When you "push" an idea into action, it never works out how you planned. If you pause and allow for inspiration, as we have suggested, and *then* you take inspired action and follow through on your intuition, your innovations will garner you great wealth, prosperity, and abundance in ALL ways, not just those you've imagined.

As you gain momentum and then plateau, that "evening-out" stage is a sign to give. As you give, you shall receive. You reap what you sow.

## Chapter 4

## *Peace On Your Planet*

As you come to know your interdependence—and you realize how different it is to meet each body's basic needs versus interfering with a person's soul agreement by judging and interfering with their lessons—you will also understand how the importance of one person's peace is crucial to world peace.

How can you be at peace when another of you, another piece of Spirit, is hungry or without shelter? How would it feel to know that every single body on earth, every representation of Spirit, has food, clothing, and a roof over their head? What would your world look like if each soul's purpose wasn't just living in survival but creating for one another in joy and Love?

This isn't to say you must provide *everything* to another, for that would indeed interfere with their purpose in coming here. And yet, as each of you has protection for your body, there will be less and less who will act out in anger and rage. Eventually, this lessening of the lower frequencies will translate into a world without war. And when there is no more war, no more separation of your so-called species, you will know "heaven on earth."

If the way station, as we call it, is an interim location—where your soul is set free to manifest at will without carrying around the density of a body—then, if this dimension becomes a place where you have *no fear* over the protection of your body, then what? Then, our friends, you are one GIANT step closer to the space where we reside.

## THE LAW OF CIRCULATION

Your body is a vast circuitry of vessels that allow the blood to run through them, yes? What do you think would happen if one of those vessels—a vein or an artery, specifically—were blocked? If your veins were dammed up, you'd likely have a heart attack or stroke or some such unpleasant thing that would terminate your lifetime as you know it.

In the same way, when you block any form of energy, it gets dammed up until it's ready to explode! When you allow fear to get in the way of what you really want, and then you get over it and DO the thing you so want to do, you call it a "breakthrough." Why? *Because you are literally breaking through your energy block.*

In terms of financial flow, this same occurrence happens, you see. When you "hoard" your income, you are literally damming up the flow! What you give, you receive. When you have the mindset that there is plenty to go around, then you create space for money and gifts and all manner of abundance to come right back to you.

So be generous. In a BIG way. Play with giving away 1%, and *watch* (time it if you must) how rapidly it returns to you. Now that you've gained some confidence in the boomerang effect of this manifestation game, try giving 10%, and watch how you get back 10 times that! And it just keeps on increasing as you gain confidence and trust and faith in the process ...

Then tell all your friends! Allow them to *see* and witness how your abundance comes back to you tenfold; share *those* positive stories instead of complaining about what is *not* coming.

What is scientifically happening, you see, is that you are creating a "vacuum." Visualize a whirlpool in the middle of an ocean or a wormhole in the middle of outer space. Abraham, the non-physical entities who communicate through Esther Hicks, would call this a "vortex," and so you see, as you give out, you are MAGNETICALLY attracting toward yourself. We'll say it again—as you give, so shall you receive. They knew of this back in biblical times.

# KNOWING PEACE

As you become a witness to this phenomena, and things, experiences, and adventures keep happening for you and to you, you will also see how giving to others creates a much BIGGER picture of peace—in your inner world as well as your outer world.

But first, we must address the question of whom you give to. Michelle's friend Amy brought this up, and we believe it is an important issue to address. The idea of "tithing" has been popular in churches for centuries. Interestingly enough, 10% of your income is usually recommended. And yet, this word has also become loaded, as many (but not all) of your churches have hoarded this revenue for themselves (creating a dam, you see) and have not allowed this money to flow freely to those in need.

We are not asking you to give it to our organization or to Michelle and Jodah, or even to "charity," which also carries with it a loaded connotation that could be conceived as akin to a victim mentality.

No, what we are saying (again) is that when every single individual on your planet does not have to fear taking care of their body—with food, clothing, shelter—your world will know peace. Our definition of peace is the opposite of fear. And if your *survival* basics are taken care of, you will not fear *others* who will try to take from you. If others are not *angry* at having their basic living needs not met, perhaps they will learn not to attack. If countries are not fighting over boundaries and misperceived power, and they understand the world's people are ONE unit, ONE Spirit, there will no longer be suffering via hunger and lack of shelter.

So ensure that no one goes homeless, naked, or hungry. Give to those projects and people who *ensure* basic survival needs for ALL! Do *not* consider the homeless less fortunate, for that is assuming you are better than they are somehow. (We are speaking to Michelle on forming a Power of 10 Peace Foundation as a hub for those who don't know where to look, and we will guide her on giving as a representative for all of you.)

Beyond food, clothing, and shelter, it is up to each individual person to RISE up and create the life they want, you see. Beyond the basics of caring for the body, it is up to each person to educate themselves properly and to learn and grow without limits! It will be much simpler to educate your people when they are not bothered by survival. Without suffering, ALL will thrive! Without bodily suffering, disease will eventually end, you see. When you care for others among you, you care for ALL!

Are you still struggling with this concept? Let us give you an example. Perhaps there is a homeless person who wanders in your area. Being in inclement weather, without proper access to cleaning apparatus, that person would likely fall prey to bacteria and/or viruses—which might find their way to YOU. Without clean, warm clothing and nutritious food for the body, that person would likely get ill. Wandering around, shunned by society, that person might lash out in anger and violence. The person on the other end of that violence might be YOU.

If you looked into the eyes of that very same person and saw the purity of their soul—the same SPIRIT that resides and animates YOU—you might find it in your heart to give freely to that person or to an organization that would help them.

Now this person is clothed, has a roof over their head, and healthy food. They make friends, find work that pleases them, and contributes to the whole. Don't you think they are less likely to strike out? And if they are less likely to strike out, you have less to fear, you see?

Not only are you getting back your dollar—or your $10,000 or $100,000 or $1,000,000, depending on how much you choose to give with FAITH that it will return to you tenfold—to spend as you wish, but you are creating heaven in the here and now. For in what you call heaven, and what we refer to as the temporary way station to the blissful space where we reside, you have no fears whatsoever because you have no body to hurt. In the same way, if *all* of your bodies do not hurt or suffer, you will know peace.

Just imagine what this might feel like! No worries for anyone about paying the rent or mortgage, or working at a job they despise, catching a disease, or fearing attack from another. No stress that your family and friends and loved ones might suffer the same "fate." No stress, no stress-related diseases or disorders. No filling a perceived void with an addictive substance because you will *know*, in Truth, there is NO VOID. As you fill the vacuum with all good things, the void you feel will become non-existent.

And now, because there are no fears or worries, what will you do with *that*?

## Chapter 5

## *Breaking Down Walls*

When enough of you lift your vibration, you will start seeing individual spirits—or "ghosts," as many call them. Everywhere.

This should not scare you in the least. You say you miss those who have passed on before you. Why do you think you say "passed on"? As in, passed on to the next level of existence? Your loved ones have simply shed their body vehicle from this particular lifetime, and their soul sped up to a rate you no longer can see as they merged with Divine Spirit.

As you speed up your frequency, many of you will be able to use your senses to feel and see and hear spirits in your midst, as Michelle has done in the past as a "medium."

You see, even your term "medium" conveys that she is a "middleman" for spirits, as she has learned to lift her vibration through meditation and various tools to reach the space where she may communicate with them. Her brief glimpse into the way station when she was younger also gave her a new perspective as to her current vibrational state and provided her with ways she could lift it higher.

This is not a "super power," as many of you believe. It is just a fact that as you raise your vibrational state, there are others higher in frequency that you may reach. You may even "pass" *them* up, as Michelle has done in reaching us.

As your vibrational state lifts, so will your intuition get stronger, to the point where it seems you know everything and ALL! This is a good thing! Perhaps a little confusing at first, as you discern where your ego lies and another's stops. You will learn better boundaries as you rise up as well, so you aren't reading everyone's minds all the time. That could be exhausting!

There are those in your midst who name this rising up "ascension," and many who associate illness and pain and other unpleasantries with the raising of your frequencies. And to that, we again say that it is only your resistance that makes it so, and as you focus on the pain and discomfort, it will only expand and get stronger! Look away from the discomfort toward the lessons it may *teach* you as you come away from learning through suffering. You are still all learning through contrast, and that is perfectly all right from your current level of understanding.

Just don't stay stuck there.

Focus on the lesson, focus on what may come of your current level of discomfort, and you'll be closer to getting there. Once you gain a momentum, your "hard" lessons should come less and less often, and you will lead a life of growth through FAITH, which is a most blissful existence.

You may lift your vibration no matter *what* is going on around you. We shall give you an example.

Michelle and Jodah went to the DMV to register the RV—the one they manifested—into their names. They had a long wait, and so Michelle brought our first book with her on her laptop to edit. And Jodah, to pass the time, read over her shoulder.

The time passed joyfully as Michelle and Jodah read the high-frequency words that lifted their vibration. Only when they took a break to give their eyes a rest did they hear all of the rampant complaining all around them.

This was amusing to them, as when they were in the "bubble" of their high-vibrational state from reading positive words, the existence of the "yolk" was not even on their radar. Rather than allowing the negativity to bring them down, they went back to editing and reading the book, and once again, they were able to block out their neighbors who were unhappy about waiting. When their number was called, the woman who helped them was extremely amicable and efficient, and they left sooner than expected.

And so, it is important each day to say *rise* as you awake in the morning to prepare you for what may come up.

## FREQUENCY LEVELS

Michelle was reading a book on manifestation and saw that the authors suggested that you only bring your frequency to the level where it matches what you want. We would beg to differ.

If you only bring your vibratory level to a specific point, you are limiting yourself. If you raise your levels a little each day, not only will it be easier on your body and mind, but you will attract things and experiences and people you didn't even *know* you wanted! Once you feel a sense of fulfillment, you'll also begin to let those levels overflow as you give to others. You will know PEACE, as we mentioned in previous chapters, because other souls—who share the same Spirit as yourself—will know peace. You will also manifest in an amplified way, making ecstasy achievable for ALL!

Limiting your manifestation levels is simply a very human way of looking at things. Don't succumb to it. You are so much MORE than you realize.

## INSTANT MANIFESTATIONS

As you realize how truly powerful you are, and your vibrational set point is at a high level, and you are attracting all manner of things on your "list" and so much *more*, you indeed must be cognizant of what you are thinking and speaking and writing.

As you lift your frequency, you see, you are speeding up the very cells rotating in your body, creating better health and vibrancy as a result. That "whirlpool" of energy you've now created will draw things and experiences to you *much* faster than in the past, where you had a "buffer" of time before your thoughts became things.

Now, much as it is in the way station, you will have a want, and it will be delivered to you almost immediately! On the flip side, you may have a fear that will *also* show up rapidly.

Michelle's friend Amy had this happen when she had the thought that she should put away an expensive vase so her children would not break it. She even had a vision of the vase broken! Yet she became distracted and forgot to put the vase in a safer location, and sure enough, her son threw a ball that hit the vase and broke it into pieces, just as in her vision!

What happened in this instance is that Amy's fear created a potential reality, and her intuition warned her of what was to come if she did not act on what was already set into motion, but she was not in present moment, and therefore, she saw her fear become a rapid reality.

Just the week prior, Amy had surpassed a different fear and sent a query to a book publisher for a parenting book she had written years ago. She sent it in and let it go without any expectations and received a rapid response to please send in the book! When she was able to surpass her fear of failure and/or judgment (so many of you have these fears; it is time to let them go!), she was rewarded with a positive outcome.

# Chapter 6

# *Holding Space for One Another*

How do you help another to manifest? That is a question running through Michelle's mind this morning as she contemplates helping her friends and family. She has given us her permission to share her stories, as they are examples of thoughts that may come across your individual minds, yes?

First, you must raise your own vibration to the highest level you can each day, without worrying about tapering off. Raise it to a point that feels powerful to you, and you will not only draw things and experiences toward yourself, you will enlighten those in your midst. As you feel good, you cannot *help* but allow those around you to feel good as well, as feeling good is contagious.

At the same time, there will be those who are of such a low vibration that they keep their distance, for your

Light may be blinding to them, you see. That is okay, as eventually ALL will learn to adjust their vision.

You cannot save another. You cannot rescue another. You *can* shine your Light for all to see by raising your vibration higher each day, as you are learning how to do in this book and in our recordings.

As like-minded friends and family share with you their new wants and desires, you may encourage them by "sharing the vision" they have for themselves. Allow them to add more details to their desires, utilizing all of their senses, and share your joy in the process! See it *with* them. Picture them in their new house, driving their new car, enjoying radiant health and vitality, sharing with others ... and so on. As you share for them, and their wish becomes a reality, they will do the same for you. You are stronger together. We have said this before, but we will emphasize it again now:

## YOU ARE STRONGER TOGETHER!

As you magnify, as you amplify, as you give out and receive in multitudes, you will rapidly gain momentum and come together. There will be no room for naysayers. They shall have their own groups, and they will be "happy" complaining and commiserating together. That is not for you. Not now. Not from here on out!

Hold the same vision for another, and see how happy it makes *you* feel. This is taking The Law of Attraction one step further, for as you learn to hold the vision for another—understanding that you are all ONE—you will create a new world, a peaceful state of humanity.

# Chapter 7

# *Peace*

You should know by now—not just intellectually but deep in your heart—that peace is an inside job. If you are not living out a peaceful existence, if your life, as you know it, is filled with stress and fear and anxiety, you are part of the problem and not the solution.

How do you live a solution-based existence? By understanding that in other dimensions the problem is already solved, and work from that point in space and time—backward, as you might "see" it.

Let us clarify. If you are in a job you hate, you find your way toward a pleasurable state that lifts your vibration until that happier state is more dominant than your familiarity toward your current painful state of existence. Until you reach that tipping point, you will continue to live in fear and resentment.

And then, as you live out your day-to-day "story," you may place blame on others because you are still too fearful to make a change in your own little world. You may blame your politicians, who are only mirroring your populace. You may blame your parents, who only came here to birth you—and it is you who continue to harbor ill will from something that happened in the past. Focus on the present, and it will no longer continue to do you harm.

You can blame anyone, really. Right now, today, Michelle was having a hard time even reaching our frequency because of the terrorist in Orlando who killed and injured so many. As an empathic soul, she is truly *feeling* the hurt and sadness and anger of the world's outrage, and she's sensing the blaming of each other in the wake of the trail of fear and madness this one man left.

Her processing of this grief is not truly doing anyone any good. She can process with compassion, and she can envision healing light over the victims of the violence, and yet—we would offer this: Peace is an inside job.

Michelle, and perhaps *you*, would do better to look for where there is "terror"—strong fear—in your own life, and work to eradicate it by knowing the Truth of who you are: Love. Fear cannot exist in a state of Love. When you die, there is no fear, only Love. Those who died at the hands of the terrorist are out of their bodies now, and they know only Love. If you act in revenge, if you step up your anger and fear, that energy wins. When it becomes dominant, you all lose.

Don't let fear become the dominant vibration in you or your people. It's simply not real. The very worst thing someone can do to you is to take your life, this one life, from you—and you will go to a place of peace and understanding, a place where your every desire is instantly manifested—and you will either heal there and come back to learn more lessons, or you will move on as we are encouraging you to do.

In the meantime, you will enact new laws, and you will write out your opinions everywhere, all in an effort to separate yourselves. The Truth is, no one can harm your soul. And, in the big picture of things, this one horrible act may propel many of you to see that you are not your gender preference, you are not your gender, you are not your age, your race, your ethnic identity. You are SPIRIT, seeking an individual soul adventure in order to expand the Universe.

You are just one very small part of an extremely huge galaxy—one of billions throughout our Universe. You cannot possibly know how small you are in reality, until you join us in Truth. Then you will just *know* that you are part of a GRAND DIVINITY that knows no boundaries.

No one is judging you. God is not a person with skin and genitals floating around in the sky. God is a force of Love, of positive growth. Again, we encourage the word "Love" rather than "God," for your separate ideologies and religious beliefs are only serving to hurt you at this point in your spiritual evolution.

If you want to stop the killing, stop the critical voice in your own mind. You are *not* powerless at all! And you are certainly not at the mercy of those you've put in charge. Stand behind your ideals, your values, and amplify HONESTY, INTEGRITY, PEACE, LOVE, COMPASSION! Then LIVE it, each and every day. Show your world Love and peace by how you act in the world—*teach by example.* Raise your vibration daily, and those in your midst will benefit. And they, too, shall raise their vibration, until that higher vibration becomes the dominant one on your planet.

With your lifted vibration, manifest more—GIVE more. Perhaps that Orlando shooter knew a life of abuse and poverty and self-hatred, which translated into him abusing his wife and taking out his anger and rage on those he cast as "other." Perhaps if that little boy had been given the basics of what he needed to survive, perhaps if he had been shown more unconditional Love and compassion, he might not have struck out.

*It is a combination of poverty and ignorance that creates violence and madness.* When you can spread your newfound, overflowing abundance with those AROUND THE WORLD, you will create well-being for ALL and a much safer space for yourselves as you finish out your days here. *Generosity and tolerance creates peace and joy ...*

## Chapter 8

## *Abundance for ALL*

Michelle was pondering what we wrote last night, about peace and moving beyond impoverished conditions. And she had the thought about why some of you act out in anger and violence, despite living in what most would consider a wealthy upbringing. She also had images floating around in her head—as she was about to drift off to sleep—of happy, joyful people who lived in what would be considered extremely poor conditions. Why are *they* so happy and not violent?

This is what we told her: "Some of the happiest, most peace-loving people in your world come from a village mentality. Think about that."

You see, it is all a matter of perception. In the first example, of a person growing up in a financially stable situation yet struggling with anger issues or other such mental constrictions—perhaps they felt as if it was never enough. Have you ever met a very wealthy person who was not happy? Sure you have. The two don't always equate, you see. If the person viewed life as "unfair" and they felt unworthy—as so many of you feel—they might harbor deep feelings of insecurity and fear and lack, despite their outward appearances.

A wealthy person may also have been indoctrinated into the belief system—which so many of you share—that says you must work *hard* to earn your income. And working hard isn't all that fun, is it? Unless, of course, you are loving what you are doing and taking inspired action based on your intuitive inclinations—that *feels* different and yields far better results.

If a person swallowed this working hard mentality and felt lazy when he or she did not accomplish something, and felt "pushed" into doing what they felt their family or society or whomever *else* expected of them, they might feel angry. And they might take out this anger on others—whether in a small or big way—especially if they felt alone in their endeavors.

Alternatively, the example of the happy yet poor villagers demonstrates how different *not* having things can feel when you are surrounded by others who help and love each other as a team. As Americans, you started out feeling this way, as if you were all in it together to experience religious freedom and tolerance. And yet, so many of you now have forgotten your origins, forgotten how it feels to SHARE, to help one another as the people of ONE WORLD, rather than the inhabitants of many separate, man-made, bordered-off sections.

What if you met somewhere in the middle? What if you had the things you need to survive *and* thrive, and you could feel as if you are creatively contributing to humanity? You *knew* that others around you *also* had the basics they needed to survive, that TOGETHER you would manifest all you need and want because you understood that what you envision for another, you also gain for yourself?

You are moving closer toward a place where there *are* no borders, no people in "charge" who represent what you want as an individual. Do you really need another WAR in order to find peace? Do you really need another WAR to create so-called "anarchy," when what you really want is harmony with one another? What if, instead of creating chaos by refusing to elect any individuals who don't represent the ideals you long for, you instilled those ideals and values from within?

Many will call this too idealistic, but that's how you began, and that's how you will be when you transcend this world. A space without borders, where everyone knows their inherent freedom and lack of limitation, is "heaven on earth." Your current way station *can* become your present reality if you let it, if you envision what you want for yourself, and make it a rapid reality then spread your intention toward another.

It can happen in your lifetime. That's why we are here. It is time for you to know this.

## Chapter 9

## *Impediments*

### JEALOUSY

Along the way, as you are gaining momentum in manifestation, and you are giving and receiving, giving and receiving, giving and receiving, you will become much like a river, in that your currents of energy will ebb and flow, ebb and flow, ebb and flow.

What might stop the free-flowing energy vibration that you long to flow WITH and not AGAINST, are a few strong emotions that act as boulders and dam up your river.

Jealousy is one of those. You know it when you feel it, because it feels almost "sticky," as if you can't wash it off. If you are feeling it toward someone, catch yourself, and turn it around into inspiration as quickly as possible! That "other" person (who is actually part of the same Spirit as you, remember?) is *demonstrating* to you what you can have, do, or be! Thank them, either internally or externally, for showing up as a reminder of what you can "vibe up" to, and then visualize yourself having, doing, or experiencing the same or better.

If you're on the other end of jealousy, please remind yourself that there are still many millions of young souls on your planet who are still in the process of spiritual evolution and who have NO idea what you are learning. Be patient with them, yet set boundaries if they attempt to use their words or actions to bring you down to their level out of fear and insecurity. They represent the yolk of the egg, remember? You are the egg white, so whip up your energy and get it all good and frothy, for there are many others who will be *inspired* by you ... And it is THOSE like-vibing people you would do well to hang out with, for as you grow in numbers, your vibrations *together* will grow exponentially.

Just watch what happens when 10 like-minded souls come together. That is how we found each other, and in the space where we reside, it is a much faster process as we are not lugging around the density of our bodies any longer. And yet, you may do it, also. Find 10 of you to get together and meet up often with the intent of having fun and just *be*-ing together, and you will find yourself much lighter and happier.

## FEELING ALONE

In the process of rising up, we must point out that there will be many others you will leave behind. This should not be such an unpleasant thing, as their energy will start to feel intolerable to you, like an itchy rash.

## CHAPTER 9 – IMPEDIMENTS

So often, you want change to happen IMMEDIATELY, and you start begging the Universe to give it to you NOW! And yet, when you are feeling signs that someone is vibrating on a different frequency as yours, you often dig your feet into the sand and refuse to budge.

You cite feeling guilty (gross). Or you feel as if you should rescue them. Maybe they do not wish to be rescued. We've been over this before, and still, you may go through this again and again as you promote yourself through various gradations of higher living.

They always have the option of rising up to meet you and the others with whom you are currently vibrating. Yet if they choose not to, please do yourself a favor, and don't label it as a "good" or a "bad" thing. You are so *good* at doing that, aren't you?

Remember, there is no good or bad. Only your judgment and perception make it so.

When you feel as if you are alone in this process, pretend to unzip your body as we have taught you in the last book, and remember who you are underneath your skin. Love and space. That is all. You can never be lonely because you are one with all of life! 7 billion souls, all choosing to come to the earth for this adventure during this particular moment in the time and space continuum. Out of 7 billion people, you should be able to find 10 like-minded individuals at any given time to grow with you ...

## RAGE

If you are still experiencing rage, you might want to revisit the first book. Anger is another matter, for it is part of being human to move fear into its more expressive form. *Anger is fear being active.* Rage takes it to another level and often propels that energy into violence. When you are feeling anger in its early stages, you may stop and witness it for what it is. Thank the emotion for showing you a blockage in your ever-flowing source of energy, and quickly deny it entrance into your river. Stop it before it causes a flood. You have the power to do this, and as you conquer anger, you show others what is possible.

## Chapter 10

## *Soaking It All In*

When do you know you are done?

This question posed itself in Michelle's head this morning. And the answer is, simply, you are *never* done. You are eternal beings of Light, and so, you go on and on and on ... Isn't that comforting?

Or is it?

If you are living out a miserable existence, a life story you wrote before you came into being that included a whole lot of conflict and drama, perhaps going on and on and on might seem awful. And so, the trick is to keep growing into your bliss, continue leaning into higher emotions and lighter vibrational states until you are manifesting daily, even moment by moment! Manifesting things, yes, but also experiences and adventures and like-vibing people and opportunities and creative projects, and—well, the list goes on and on, doesn't it?

And yet, that doesn't matter, because you do not have an expiration date! From here, you go on manifesting, and from that place of rampant health, wealth, Love and *overflowing* abundance, you GIVE. You give 1% of your incoming goodness, then 10%, then ALL of it, and you WATCH gleefully as it returns to you tenfold!

You see, this "game" of life you chose can be so much fun with the right focus and attention to what MATTERS! You matter. You *make* things matter. You make things *into* matter. Get it?

As your creations overflow to other peoples, *your* people (because you understand innately now that you are indeed ONE SPIRIT, expressing itself through differing souls) you create first a community, then a *world* where no one need suffer. You feel GOOD, knowing that the other souls expressing your same Light are not going hungry somewhere "out there." You feel fantastic, knowing they have the basics for their survival; they are clothed, fed nutritious foods, and have clean, solid shelter, and so further growth and creation is up to them. Because you understand how to manifest instantaneously, as you walk among them they will feel your peace and light up, too! They will learn by your example—and by the example of those you've already magnetically gathered amongst you—that *they, too,* can create by using their imaginations and intuition and inspired action!

Soon, you will find your way station is HERE! And from here, you don't even have to reach higher, you see, because there is no "higher" and "lower." That was only a construct of your mind while you perceived limitation and dense matter. As your frequency rises, as you literally "speed up," you will move BEYOND needing and wanting things, because you will already enjoy the *freedom* and *bliss* that were behind those "things" and experiences all along!

You will literally float around all day and night—not even needing sleep as your body is revved up so high it does not need recharging—and so you travel around this very beautiful planet of yours, admiring it and feeling great gratitude for it. You wander in appreciation, spreading your positive vibes wherever you go, like seedlings.

When you do decide to shed this body, it will be the easiest transition possible, because you will already be of the Light. Your vibe will be so close to where we are, it will only be what you call a "hop, skip, and a jump" to where we reside.

We can't wait to meet you here!

In fact, Michelle is "buzzing" because she feels our excitement and enthusiasm for where you all are already, just by reading and hearing these words! Keep reading and re-reading, continue to listen to the recordings and watch the videos until you feel higher than happy. Because there is a place that is higher than what you consider "happy," we promise.

We are now coming to the end of this first section of the book. There will, of course, be many more. Step beyond now into each lesson. Perhaps read one a day, or one each week, and follow through on practicing the tools. Meet together in groups to discuss how things are changing for you and those in your midst. We love being your teachers, and we love seeing how many of you are attracted to the teachings because you recognize Truth when you feel it. Keep sharing, and soon you will know peace.

# Step Beyond

## Lesson #1: Step into the Light

Find a ray of light, or a band of sunshine, streaming through your window or into your yard. If it's raining, wait for the rain to end, and be patient for a bit of sun to come out. When you do, stand in the rays while bathing in the source of who you truly are. Imagine those rays of light washing away any doubts or fears, any worries or stress, any resentment or anger. Perhaps ask for assistance from a Divine being who is also one with the Light—an angel or spirit guide or ascended master. You may ask us, as The Power of 10, to surround you as well, for we love you and will always come to you when you raise your frequency in such a way.

Take your time with this. Within the light it will feel as if time stops, for again, that is the Truth of your existence. There is no time. And so, bathe in the light for several minutes until you feel lighter, happier, more at peace.

## Lesson #2: Peace Challenge

We understand the challenge of existing and creating and yes—thriving—in a dense environment such as yours. And yet, at a deeper level you *chose* it in order to overcome its perceived obstacles.

One of your most powerful tools—indeed, it could be called a "superpower"—that you've all been given inside your bodies is the ability to think with your mind and to have those thoughts turn into your reality.

Again, we know you know this by now, and so we'd like you to take it a step further today in an effort to "speed up" world peace. We know it is something you are keenly aware of due to the contrast of the rampant violence in your news and on your mind.

Today, we'd like to challenge you to "keep your peace." We do not mean this as in keeping your mouth shut, as the phrase is often used, but to see and watch and witness how long you can go without having a negative, critical, or even violent (against yourself or others) thought.

You could be going along with your day, and suddenly, an ugly thought from your past surfaces, or an angry song lyric, or a judgment on another. Don't get mad at yourself when it happens—that would defeat the purpose of this exercise! Rather, time how long you can go before one of these thoughts surface. Log it by writing it down, and see if—by your simple, loving awareness—you can allow more and more time to go between such thoughts that bring down your vibration.

As the thought arises, acknowledge it, and just as rapidly wipe it away. Know that it is an illusion. Share this experience with others, and soon, you'll notice an energetic difference in your intimate circles. When this happens, you are creating a "stirring of the force" that others can feel across the world, even across the Universe!

In these small, personal triumphs, you first learn—then teach—peace.

## LESSON #3: RAISING YOUR CONSCIOUSNESS

We came to you during this period of time and space that has become a vast playground—or as many see it, a battleground—of contrast. And yet, we would like to remind you that this world of yours is ALL an illusion. All of it! It is a "figment" of your imagination—you creating your life story, much of it as you go.

Many of you are fighting right now over the American political system, which *you* created. Your political representatives serve as a *mirror* for all of your collective ideals and values.

We can hear you saying right now that they are not *your* ideals and values, and yet the opposite would be true, or they wouldn't be showing up in "people" form.

Everything before you is your own manifestation.

If there are those in what you see as a place of "power" who are symbolizing lower vibratory states of consciousness, such as hate and greed, you must ask yourself where are you experiencing and/or expressing these denser egoic emotions in your own life?

If everything is Spirit, and that is a prerequisite belief for what we are teaching you, then what you are experiencing and expressing as an individual soul is showing up for you to heal and learn from—NOT by throwing temper tantrums like a small child—but by seeing the lower emotion and learning how to transform it rapidly before it gains momentum, as we have taught previously.

When you watch the news, do you feel uplifted and empowered, or dejected and powerless? When you listen to angry music, ask yourself how you feel afterward? On a scale of 1 to 10, much like they use in many hospitals, how would you rate your current level of consciousness? How does it change before and after your choices of what you watch, what you listen to, what you feed your body and soul? Would your stick-figure face be smiling and joyous, or angry and filled with anguish?

How might you lift your current level of consciousness, perhaps to just the next level up? Write down some examples of things, food, people, songs, and places that make you feel good, and incorporate them into your life this week. Then write down how you felt before and afterward. Keep a log of this, and soon you will be making better choices. As YOU make better choices, so will those around you, and as you radiate Love, peace, and happiness, these emotions and values will spread like a positive contagion. Eventually, as more and more of you wake up to your inherent oneness and the power by which you can transform humanity's ideals by uplifting your OWN internal awareness, the more your people in places of power will mirror the same.

Eventually, you will no longer need individuals in places and seats of "power," for you will all realize your inherent power. Do you think we elect souls? That went away a long, long time ago ... along with our need to reincarnate into new bodies.

## Lesson #4: Diamond Dust

As Michelle was lying in bed last night, drifting into sleep, her body felt tingly all over. At first, she had the thought that her blood circulation was being cut off, but there was no position in her body that would make that so.

We told her to imagine she's made of Diamond Dust—that all of those "tingles" were shimmers of sparkling light, because in Truth, that's what you are made of. Perhaps it is a little easier for you to envision diamonds because they are of a more solid matter, closer to your current level of density than to that of pure light.

This is a most powerful visual, seeing your "body" made up of Diamond Dust, especially if your body is currently experiencing an illness or injury. Please remember how powerful your mind is and how this world you see is all your perception. See yourself made of Diamond Dust, and then of the light that reflects from the diamonds ... there, how does that feel?

Now of course, AMPLIFY times 10! Enjoy the tingles.

## Lesson #5: Syncing Up Frequencies

There are going to be times in your process of lifting your vibration and building energy when you will surpass those around you who used to share a similar vibration.

Think of it as your cells, and the very atoms inside of those cells, bouncing around faster. Your cells, while more vibrant, are no longer a match for those you've grown to love, and that's okay. Perhaps, being in your midst, they may also get a higher "charge." Sometimes, all that bouncing around may irritate them as they resist change. That is not your process.

Your only journey—we've said it before and will repeat it numerous times until you understand fully—is to lift your own vibration a little more each day. Rise. Amplify. Ignite. Expand.

And yet, there is indeed a process you may use to "sync up" with your friends and family who are already positive and of like mind.

Imagine your mind is like a Bluetooth. That is a good visual for you at this moment in time, yes? Go ahead and picture your electronic devices beeping and lighting up, or whatever it is they do by the time you read this. Tell your mind to "sync up" with those closest around you. It won't work if they are strongly resistant to change or if they are too far apart from you, but it will work if you two are just a little "off."

If you find you no longer resonate with another soul, please make a conscious effort to let go of your attachment to them. Allow them to live out their own soul agreements, and trust that soon you will attract new souls with whom to interact.

You may feel lonesome in this process. Loneliness is relieved when you attract those who understand your vibe because they are "*there.*" How can you be lonely when you understand and *live* from your state of oneness? There are 7 billion of you at this time, experiencing the same planet, with widely varying levels of knowing. Be with those whose frequencies you match, and you will engage in a more harmonious existence.

Try syncing up as an experiment, whether it is with a spouse, a partner, a friend, a child. Write down the results so you remember. In this way, you may sync up one soul at a time, until the point where you are ALL lifted and engaged!

## Lesson #6: Beyond Belief

Abraham has taught that a belief is simply a thought you think over and over again.

And so, if you have been practicing this understanding until you DEMONSTRATE that you are living it, how can you then move *beyond* it to a state of complete faith, trust, and surrender?

Today's lesson is, when something "comes up" for you that you see as a challenge or obstacle, we encourage you to affirm:

**I am beyond this** [insert illness, lack of job, partner, friends, finances] **limiting circumstance.**

How does it FEEL when you move beyond?

Michelle was feeling the beginnings of a migraine before one of our events, and so she practiced our words and tools until her vibration was such that she no longer felt the physical pain of the migraine.

It returned the next day, and she again utilized the word "rise" until she no longer felt the suffering of the migraine, and she traced the thought that led up to her belief in suffering, and she reminded herself, "I now learn through FAITH and NOT suffering" and thus, wiped the "slate" of her mind clear.

In the same way, once you do this on a regular basis, you may move beyond your limited ego and personal thoughts and belief systems to the following new way of understanding:

The very definition of your politics and religion is an organized belief system. What if you *dis*-organized? *Dis*-engaged? Would that create chaos? What *is* chaos, anyway? What if you moved *beyond* the belief system—in the same way you have learned to move beyond your personal beliefs—knowing that beliefs are simply thoughts you choose to think over and over again. Belief *systems*, in this way, are thoughts you've been *fed* over and over again.

THIS is the way to peace, friends—this un-engaging from the thoughts and belief systems you've been fed since birth—and even *beyond* birth into other lifetimes.

When is it going to stop? When you can cease all thoughts flowing through the mind, whether through meditation or by being in the flow of movement, or by using some such tool until you LIVE from this space, you can also be 100% free of the thoughts you've been fed throughout your many lifetimes. Remember, a belief is only a thought you think over and over again. Stop the madness. Be free.

Opt out and be free.

## Lesson #7: Love Activated

As we have said previously, you do not need to manufacture Love. You do not even need to find Love. Love is the very root of your being. The Universe is made up of Love, and you are a part of the Universe, as is everyone else.

And so, in order to activate Love, you only need to remove the thoughts and belief systems that have told you that you were unlovable.

Deep down, you know this as Truth. How can you be unlovable if you are made up of Love? That makes no sense.

One way to do this activation is to start more of your sentences with "I love …" In the past, you may have started your sentences—or even your thoughts prior to speaking your sentences—with "I hate the way that …" or "It bothers me when …" or "I'm afraid that …"—therefore creating an unwanted reality.

Instead, catch yourself at the beginning of the thought, and change it to "I love …" and allow your brain to fill in the blanks of what it is you have to be grateful for. The more often you do this, the more you will wake up with "I love …" in your head, and you will live from this space of who you truly are, which is the very definition of being authentic.

## Lesson #8: My Greatest Manifestation List

It is a great Truth that what you focus on expands. And so, as you search your memory bank for things, people, experiences, opportunities, ideas, and adventures you have successfully manifested from the ethers of your mind into reality, you will only create more. As your "fountain" of manifested goods and services overflows, you will be able to give as much as you receive, if not more ...

Today's lesson involves placing "greatest manifestation" in your mind's "Google search." What comes up for you? *Nothing* is not an option. If you have a child, that is a beautiful manifestation. If you have a pet, a job, a house—you get the picture. If you imagined it, and it revealed itself to you, you created it. And as a creator, you are wise to remember and expand ...

Please take the time to make a list of at least 10. Remember, "great" doesn't necessarily have to mean "large." After a recent workshop, Michelle went to the restroom during the break, and no one else was in that section of the hotel at the moment, but a staff person with a basket full of chocolates and pens asked her if she wanted any, and then she gave her "seconds"!

Now, anyone who truly knows Michelle understands how much she loves chocolate! And pens, well, she is an author and always on the lookout for them. It *shows* you what happens when you lift your vibration so high that people just want to give you things. Little or big, doesn't really matter. You all manifest for each other when you serve by shining examples.

On the way out, Michelle realized her watch battery was dead (*we keep reminding her that there's no such thing as time, as it is all an illusion*), and she had no idea what time it was and couldn't find a clock in the lobby. Just then, two young men walked by, and one said, "Dude, Starbucks is closed? What time is it?" And she had her answer...

Those are just two very small examples of great manifestations. Make your list in your journal now.

## LESSON #9: NOTHING IS IMPOSSIBLE

No *thing* is impossible. Everything is possible.

As you have learned from the last exercise, as a creator, you have created many, many things from your most powerful thoughts. You, simply put, are amazing! If you can create all those things, think of how many *more* things you may create going forward—for yourself *and* your loved ones *and* the world?

By deductive reasoning, if you have created all those things, then no "thing" is impossible, is it? And if no thing is impossible, then EVERYTHING IS POSSIBLE.

Imagine *that*! No, please do ...

How do you feel now that you've learned that everything is indeed possible?

Share your findings with like-minded others on the same path as you, perhaps through a Power of 10 gathering taught by a certified Power of 10 instructor. Continue to share your greatest manifestations, and those that came *after* you listed out your greatest manifestations! And when you come to the place where you have no doubts, no fears, no worries, you will *live* through trust and faith and LOVE, which is the most powerful way in which you may vibrate.

You are becoming a giant magnet for good. That is *good*, yes?

That is all.

## LESSON #10: SAVOR LIFE'S EXPERIENCES

So many of you rush through your lives, inhaling each experience as if it were your last. Since you view life as limited, it presents itself to you in this way. If you were to view life as we see it, as a great continuum of eternality, you might learn to savor each adventure and lesson in your dimension, knowing there is much, much more …

Stop checking things off your "bucket list." There is no bucket. You have experienced many, many lifetimes and gone through so many lessons! Now it's time to savor each moment, even the very minute ones you now deem mundane. Being alive is special. It is unique in its level of density. Your life—your world—is the clay, and you are the artist. Play with it, sculpt it, smooth it over—or start over. You can do with it as you will.

Imagine a piece of chocolate slowly melting in your mouth. If you were hungry, you might swallow it nearly whole, without enjoyment of the varying tastes. If you were full and satisfied, you might take your time with it, feeling it roll over your tongue, perhaps even closing your eyes to heighten your tasting senses.

In this way, from a state of life fulfillment and the wisdom and knowledge that your soul is eternal, slow down and enjoy your beautiful moments. If you find you are always in a rush and your current choices reflect this hurried state, make some changes. Now. You won't regret it. Things may "speed up" where we reside, but we are in the constant center where there is complete and utter peace. Be like us.

## Lesson #11: Frequency Changes

It is not a "bad" marriage, a bad job, a bad friendship—it is simply a case of relationships that no longer match in vibrational frequency. Move on in order to achieve harmony. Stop telling yourself you are learning from all the contrast. You may have learned in the beginning stages, but now you have just formed an unhealthy attachment.

## Lesson #12: Heartbreak and Loss

If you are feeling heartache over the death or killing of another—good! That means you are feeling compassion and empathy toward that soul, who comes from the same Source Spirit! But please don't feel sorry for them, as they have already achieved a higher vibrational alignment than you. Instead, ask them to sync up with you in your current state of density, that you might rise closer to where they now reside in the way station and beyond—a place where you might achieve their same levels of peace and understanding.

## Lesson #13: Your Systems are Breaking Down

Your current system of economics is based on the "haves" and the "have nots." This fosters a sense of separation and competition, yes? Those deemed "not strong enough" are mocked and often left to die.

When your system is based on the "haves" AND the "haves," everyone wins! You must do whatever it takes to level the playing field and start anew, for this separation is entrenched in your mind, but not in your soul. Your soul knows better. Your soul feels GOOD when it is engaged in cooperation and generosity and kindness.

As you witness your current financial systems breaking down, and you fear chaos, please remember that most of you are still in the early stages of learning through suffering rather than from faith. From the contrast, you will exact how much healing needs to take place. As decade and even centuries-old doctrines, laws, and regulations that don't make sense in your day and age fall apart, you will create new guideposts for living free that includes ALL sentient beings.

When you align more with the falling-apart system that is not working for you, rather than a new system that brings hope and guidance and freedom, you will sink down with the yolk of your humanity. RISE UP, and know that a new way awaits you—a way of being that is much closer to the way station and beyond, where you may manifest for each other in harmony and peace and understanding!

You change your phones and computers in America more often than you do your laws. Don't you think it's time for an upgrade?

## Lesson #14: A New Guidance System

Many of you, if not all of you, are running on systems and documents that were created hundreds, even *thousands*, of years ago. Do you think this is very intelligent of you?

We will take your American Constitution as an example. Your "founding fathers" were well intentioned, and they even put into writing ways that the document could be amended as time wore on and things changed. And yet, there were many, many things that they could never have foreseen, given their current belief systems.

How can you create a system of checks and balances, let's say, if you are a slave owner and believe that it is okay to own another human being? How can you create a system of rules and regulations that does not include half of your population (women)? Did they foresee a future that included this population? Maybe, but their writings sure did not include them.

And your Bible, upon which many of you base most of your most heartfelt, fundamental ideals—why would you follow a document that says you should be stoned to death, for any reason?

It is time to draft new documents that outline the state of your world in this moment in time and space, and perhaps redraft it every year or so as you evolve. Form partnerships, in which you outline a new vision for your leaders and overall guidelines, and watch how they step up to meet them. You all make it so complicated. The number one rule you should all follow would be to be kind to one another. That should be a given, since you *are* one another in Spirit.

At the root of most political and religious systems is the idea that you are ONE. It is written on your American dollar—in an old, unused language, of course. It's time for an upgrade, but we foresee all your systems crashing before you truly understand this notion. There is nothing to be afraid of during this "crashing." After the storm will come the calm. Out of seeming chaos will a new world be built—one based on faith and not fear.

## Lesson #15: Everything is Happening Now

For you see, everything you could ever want or hope for is all happening NOW, at the same time!

There IS no past or future, there is only always the now. All dimensions are occurring simultaneously—and so, if you are experiencing something less than savory, you are simply not tapping in to your highest Self, your highest concept of your world.

Every single day, when you rise in the morning after a good night's rest, you may affirm that you are living your highest and best Self, and it will be so.

After you get the hang of this, and you watch your life respond accordingly, you may practice affirming the highest and best world—one that knows only peace without suffering.

Do this until it becomes a part of your vibration, and you no longer need to put it into words or even actions. Your vibration will attract everything it needs, based on this new "filter" you've put on your body vehicle, as it acts as a magnet for your perceptions.

Understand that what you want IS ALREADY HAPPENING. Do you truly get this?

Meditate on it until you do, then act accordingly.

## LESSON #16: PART OF YOUR SOUL

Now that you understand that all occurrences and experiences are happening simultaneously, you may comprehend that if your soul is untethered and a part of Spirit, and Spirit is unlimited and can be in more than one body, more than one place at once, then a part of your soul may very well *already* be in the way station and even beyond ...

Sit with that a moment.

If you can know this as your Truth, really know and understand this wisdom, you may now create a magnetic vibration that syncs up to your highest Self in the way station and beyond—a dimensional space where you may manifest at will, heal your soul's past life traumas and learn from them, and move on to a dimension that knows no fears or desires. Where we reside, there is only peace and bliss, and as you learn to float around in this space without creating problems and drama for yourself, you will radiate a peace and understanding that is contagious.

It is this sort of peaceful contagion that we encourage.

The only reason you do not reside in this blissful peace and calm is that you believe you are not worthy of such great Love. Please remember, you are made of such unconditional Love. You are born from it and into it—it is who you are throughout all levels of dimensions and lifetimes. Affirm it until you live from it. Anyone in your life who has ever told you differently is telling a lie and projecting their belief systems on you from a flawed premise. If your parents, or your siblings, or teachers, or friends, or boss ever told you something that caused you to believe you were less than perfect, it is only because *they* themselves felt less than.

EVERYTHING IS A PROJECTION. Your world is a hologram. What you see is but a mere reflection of your soul's mirror.

How do you change that image? Tell yourself the Truth every day until it "sinks in." You are indeed Divine Source energy, inhabiting form—you and everyone else on your planet. Those who you love who have "died" and left their body vehicles are now Divine Source energy, NOT inhabiting a form. That is the only difference.

Stop focusing on the outer form, but rather the TRUTH of your inner substance. That's where the magic happens.

## LESSON #17: COMPARE OR CONTRAST

When you focus on that which you don't like—in yourself or another or a situation—you create MORE of it.

We all live in a positive, creation-based Universe that knows no lack.

Up until now, you have chosen to learn in this dense reality from contrast—the very opposite of what you wanted.

You had to know fear before you knew peace.

You had to know violence before you knew peace.

You had to know hate before you knew peace.

And yet, all of those contrasting emotions and experiences led you to one conclusion—inner and outer peace, yes?

And so, why would you keep on learning through contrast? You've been told that's all there is, to just "get used to it" because it would ALWAYS be a part of your reality. And we are here to say that is old news.

Stop creating the contrast. Learn your lessons. Affirm and bring in the vibration that you are filled with integrity, generosity, courage, compassion, etc., and you will no longer have to learn the hard way!

Many of you wish to remember your past lifetimes. We say, that is all in the past (which is all happening right now, anyway)! What would you have learned from those lifetimes? Please write down all the qualities you hope your soul has learned by now, after all these lifetimes. It's time to stop flunking out and to graduate into new ways of being that are HOPE based. To do otherwise is to stay mired in unhappiness and misery. We are here to teach you how NOT to be that way. It is time to RISE, friends. Rise, Rise, RISE, and ignite your enthusiasm for this adventure! RISE UP!

## Lesson #18: You Create Your Own Problems

You see, every single problem or obstacle you've ever seen is your conception.

When you fear, you create situations in which to fear. When you are angry, you create violence. When you are resentful, you create sickness for your body vehicle. When you doubt, you interfere with your soul's purpose to remember its true nature—LOVE.

When you ask how you get in your own way, this is it. We are NOT saying to *not* have these emotions. Bottling them inside will only serve to also get in your own way. We *are* saying to acknowledge those feelings are there, and to choose a new feeling rapidly before that emotion gains momentum and attracts a less-than-positive result.

For instance, you awake with a neck ache. Perhaps you slept all night with your neck in one position that was not conducive to a pain-free existence. It happens in your dense reality. Notice it, perhaps rub it, and change your schedule that day to allow for rest and relaxation. Maybe receive a massage, or do some stretching, and then move on the following day to a pain-free existence.

Alternatively, you could wake up and tell yourself how awful it is that you woke up with this neck pain. You could *cause* a lot of suffering by choosing thoughts that back up why your life sucks and is filled with pain. You might get up and then stub your toe, thereby justifying these thoughts. The sink may not work now because you are creating a filter of "my life is full of pain and suffering" rather than "my neck hurts today, and therefore, I will take better care of myself today."

Do you see and understand the difference?

## LESSON #19: ALLOW THE WORLD TO SYNC UP

As you learn to sync up to those around you, and as you learn to live in high vibrational harmony with yourself without the need for tools—with just the pure power of presence and the knowledge and inner wisdom that you are Divine Love incarnate—you can *allow* the earth to sync UP to your now-higher vibrational alignment.

This does *not*, however, mean you must carry the world upon your shoulders. Quite the contrary: when you are in a state of surrender and allow the closest vibrational levels to rise up to meet yours, everyone wins, and everyone of a higher consciousness will feel the subtle—yet powerful—differences.

If you've gotten this far, and you are feeling daily of a high vibrational nature, you have already "synced up" with your highest Self—the best and highest version of You. It should feel like pure BLISS! If you've read this far and are not finding yourself *living* in this state, please go back and re-read our first book.

If you are not here already, please do not chastise yourself for not being ready. That kind of critical thinking will only serve to sink you back down again, and you will not become the Light of the world you were meant to be! Repeat this course and its helpful tools, lessons, and emotional/spiritual guideposts until you feel the difference.

Michelle woke up this morning at 6 a.m. and wrote for a solid two hours, allowing our words to pour through her into her typing hands. She then did some yoga for grounding, followed by a most elevating meditation, and then a naked soak in her hot tub. She is fasting today, to maintain her lighter density, and her heart is palpitating noticeably from the higher vibration. She has elevated substantially, and she is feeling it in the density of her body. We have instructed her to have no reaction to this higher state, other than welcoming it in. It is part of the path that leads to a higher plane of existence for her, as well as for all others, for you are ALL connected. You are ALL ONE. Rise and UNITE! You are not LIFTING the world, per se; you are lifting your soul-Self, and therefore, all of humankind.

## Lesson #20: Peace Principles

Peace is not just the absence of violence. It has movement, in and of itself.

You cannot have peace in your external world until you find peace within you. Your life, your world, is a hologram of your thoughts and words. When you have eradicated all criticism, judgment, and harshness in your vocabulary, you will no longer see it reflected before you.

When enough of you practice this regularly, you will know peace in your friendships. When you see peace in your friendships, it will spread rapidly throughout your community and into your city, your state, your country, and beyond.

It starts with vision. You must *want* peace before peace can begin. Many of you still attach to fear, doubt, resentment, and so forth. Purge your soul of these emotions, and you will move forward as a people.

When you see others in your news strike out and hurt and kill, raging and retaliation are never the response. When you feel empathy toward both the killer and the killed, the murderer and the murdered, the maimer and the maimed, (because you were once all of them in one life or another!) and SHOW them how peace is maintained, it *will* spread.

Focus on the good, and you will see more good. Your life is all about which lens and filters you place on it.

Hug and touch each other with Love. When you discard this particular body vehicle, you will understand how much this was one of the primary reasons you chose this adventure again—to FEEL. When you refrain from human touch, you separate from each other, and you both lose. If you were never shown affection in your childhood, this is even more true.

Be independent, as well as interdependent. What this means is that when you are in charge of many of your basic needs, you don't have to depend on others and therefore blame another when it is not going as planned. Live in smaller surroundings, own your house in full, grow your own food, make your own clothing or wear recycled clothes. Simplify your life, and make more of your moments count. It will FEEL as if you are living longer, because you are not rushing through life in blame and judgment. Make your life your own. Create it from where you are.

Eat organically. No more excuses. If you go to a large box of a grocery store, understand that there will be preservatives and insecticides used to make the food last longer and look pretty so you will buy it. Even if you must pay a little more to get organic, it always pays in the long run, for you are basically choosing between "poisoned" and "un-poisoned." Even when you go directly to the farmer, be sure to ask if they farm organically. In this way, over time, you will eradicate your diseases. Wouldn't life be more fun and peaceful without disease? It starts with your food consumption. And once you are able to eat organically for yourself, consider sharing a bag of food with another who has none. If "they" are no longer at risk for disease, they will not spread it to you, and you both win. You have helped a fellow soul, *and* you have helped your own body-self. This earth has everything you ever want to feed and nourish you. So SHARE. You should have been taught that as a child, yes? If not, learn it as an adult, and pass it on ...

Never stay stuck. Move your body daily, and explore your world in all of its beauty. The more of you who travel to other locations, the more you will see people intrinsically are the same everywhere you go! The outer beauty changes, as it also does in you, but you all share the same Spirit. Observe how souls creatively express themselves. Admire how differently they choose to do so, and yet, you all love, you all have experienced hardships, and you all seek pleasure and beauty and goodness. You all eventually must "die" to this kindergarten-like existence, and most of you have reincarnated thousands of times. Hopefully, now, most of you will choose to move on to the place where we reside and beyond us! But for now, realize that *all* of your borders are manmade. Just like "time" and "space," your "borders" are all an illusion, used to separate and define you by a conglomeration of ego-centric minds. You are one people. It's time to act like it. Travelling is important to achieving long-lasting peace.

## LESSON #21: ONCE YOU COMMIT, IT BECOMES YOURS

So many of you say you want something, but you are—as you say—"wishy-washy" in your desires.

Until you have made up your mind and offer a steady frequency, the Universe cannot match the vibration of your desire. Another way to say this is, once you commit, it is already yours.

How do you do that, you say? You simply decide, and then believe in yourself 100%. Continue to imagine already having what it is you want, and it is already yours in another higher dimension. Match up with that higher dimension, and you bring it into this one.

It does not matter whether it is an object or an experience; it is the commitment that brings it to you.

If it is a person you want, however, they have their own commitments and desires, and so if they match, you will come together. If you do not vibrate at the same frequency, you two will *not* come together. Do not sit around waiting until this lines up, because you may be waiting for an eternity. Your life is happening NOW.

If you want love, affirm you *are* Love, and those who love you will line up for you, whether it is in your romantic relationships, friendships, career contacts, children, etc.

If you want money, what you really want is freedom. And so, rightfully affirm that in Spirit, you are always free. And watch how examples of freedom—and yes, money, but also inspiration and travel, creative opportunities and adventure—show up for you!

And if you want peace, you must clear your mind and heart of any negativity, and *be* peace. As you live from this perfect space of kindness, generosity, and clearheadedness, the world will show you more examples of peace.

If you haven't yet decided what it is you want, or if you are still clarifying, that is okay, also. But don't expect it to show up for you until you are fully committed.

## LESSON #22: OUTRAGE AND VIOLENCE

If you feel outrage over violence, you then become a part of the problem and not the solution. The answer is to look deep within and wipe out any feelings of anger or rage. *The world is reflecting your emotions, remember? You are a hologram, remember?* When you feel anger, switch it with peace. When you feel fear, switch it with faith. Conjure up images in your mind that demonstrate peace and faith and Love, and this will reflect in your outer world. React with pain, and you'll create more suffering. React with more rules and regulations, and you'll restrict your very own freedom! Stop the madness. Go within and switch it up.

If you die before you finish this process, remember that your soul never dies. It just merges with Pure Presence. You will *know* peace when you leave this body behind. Those who lost their lives in whatever tragedy you are thinking about right now—THEY KNOW PEACE. Do not mourn for them, because they know more about peace right now than you do. Sync up to them, in their now-high vibrational reality that does not judge or condemn, with your peaceful intentions. Harmonize higher to know peace, and peace will be yours.

## Lesson #23: See Souls, Not Bodies

Hopefully you have practiced the exercise we taught you in the last book—to look into another's eyes and see one another's souls. If not, we suggest you try this with a friend, spouse, pet, child, or other such close living being first.

Then, having garnered the intimacy that comes with such practice, we would like you now to branch out, and look into the eyes of anyone you encounter today. You do not even have to speak to them; just see past their skin, past their gender, their cultural identity, and see them as the soul they are—the soul that shares the very same Spirit as you do.

They may look at you funny, at first, but that's okay. If they ask what you are doing and why you are looking at them that way, just tell them the truth—that you are practicing looking past any judgments—and tell them they are beautiful. Because in Truth, all souls are beautiful, aren't they?

See *past* the differences today, look *beyond* any surface beauty or perceived imperfections to the shiny soul behind them. Once this practice feels comfortable to you, you may play with it beyond this one day. However, you do not need to. Once you've done this for a good 24 hours, you will be changed forever. You will never see another person the same way again.

## Lesson #24: Vocabulary

Please strike the following from your vocabulary: *I need, I miss, I want …*

There are many more, but let's start there. When you use such words, it implies "lack of," when in Truth, you lack nothing. Everything you've ever thought you wanted or needed is already yours; you just haven't brought yourself to the same consistent frequency of it to bring it into this dimension, and therefore, into your vision and experience.

When you say, "I miss \_\_\_\_," it implies that you wish the past were in the present, or that a person who has moved on, either spiritually or emotionally, is *not* in Truth connected to you anymore. You are always connected, even in your so-called "death," because you are all one, and because you shared an emotional connection. A part of their soul is always with you, so in fact, you miss nothing.

Your thought is a thing, a force. Your words speak your thoughts, and so they become even more powerful. With each word you think and say you are, in effect, casting a spell upon the world that you see. Spells are not "evil," as you have labeled them. Why do you think you use the same word to spell out a word as you do for casting a magic spell? They come from the same origin, and so again, we would like you to use your words wisely. Think before you say them, and say them deliberately.

Create a list now in your journal or on a piece of paper or an electronic device of words you may use in place of: I need, I miss, I want. If you can't think of any, sit in meditation until they come to you, or say out loud the following affirmation:

I am all that I could ever need or want.

I have everything, for I AM everything.

I am connected to everyone and everything, and I am ever present in my eternal NOW.

Now how does *that* feel? Repeat often or daily.

## LESSON #25: MEDITATION IS ACTION

When faced with a perceived obstacle to your peace, often you have a knee-jerk reaction to whatever is happening before you. You say, "But I need to DO something." "I must stop THEM from doing this [thing]." *Does that feel peaceful to you?*

We will remind you again that EVERYTHING IS ENERGY, YOU ARE ALL CONNECTED, and YOUR THOUGHTS CREATE YOUR REALITY. If you truly believe this in your heart, then clearing your mind in meditation—or a meditative flow of action—is indeed *doing* something! In fact, it is the very *best* thing you could do in a stressful situation. You are adding peace to the collective unconscious instead of fear or anger or some such harmful emotion. As you contribute peace to the overall "bank" of souls, you will see your world unfurl before you. There are as many examples of peace as there are of violence—it is all a matter of what you place your focus on.

Your journalists write a fear-based story, and their "numbers" rise, and their bosses take notice. The people who advertise also take notice, and so the journalists are asked to focus on yet another fear-based story, so people, such as you, take notice and read it and react. *They want you to react.* And you are doing exactly what they want you to do.

A better response, we would suggest, would be to *not participate. A better response would be non-reaction—in other words, peace.* You may practice this on a smaller scale in your individual lives. If someone wants to inflict their insecurities on you by their behavior, if you engage, the negative behavior escalates. If you choose to not participate, the negativity dissipates.

When you are parenting a small child, if you yell at them for perceived misbehavior, they might yell louder by your example, and now you are in a screaming match for attention. If you would choose to look the other way and find a better-feeling vibration, they would match your new frequency.

Looking the other way is *not* passive. It is simply not adding fuel to the fire. Stop adding to the violence on your planet by taking sides in an argument. There is only one side—Spirit. Taking sides is yet another form of ego separation. Stop contributing to it if you want to truly know peace, inside *and* out.

And while we're at it, stop telling other people what to do. *Do you like being told what to do?* Neither does anyone else. Light yourself up from the inside out, and others will be sure to take notice! Lead by your shining example of integrity, honesty, kindness, generosity, and faith, and you will do more good than any other action you could take.

## Lesson #26: I am Peace

But what if you are in the midst of a perceived threat or fight or some unpleasant interaction that has you all topsy-turvy in your emotional state? What if, in the midst of this trauma you are suffering for yourself in order to learn, you just can't find a calm state in which to meditate, as your mind is a turbulent sea, as if in a storm?

Michelle was in this state just yesterday when she got into a dispute with her teenage daughter. She was in tears, her mind kept telling stories that weren't true, and she was taking it all very personally, despite her deeper knowledge to the contrary.

Please remember: you are all still living in a very dense environment, where you placed yourself in order to learn through contrast. In fact, it is still the very best way for you to learn, despite the pain it may cause you. The pain may be inextricable from the experience, and yet, we would offer that the suffering is quite optional. You create the suffering by your resistance to the "what is."

In the midst of her turmoil, when Michelle could not sleep, we whispered to her the Truth of her being: "I am peace."

Not "I *want* peace." That is quite different, yes? At the core of your being, you ARE peace! You are made of it. Like Love, it is not something to achieve or desire—it is who you really are. And so, if you find yourself in a state of suffering, we advise to affirm that you *are* peace. Say it over and over and over again until you achieve a state of calm, or at least your mind stills some.

Say it now:

I am peace.

I AM peace.

Peace is who I truly am.

In my heart of hearts, I KNOW I am peace.

I am now calm.

My mind is still and calm.

I am peace.

## Lesson #27: Look for the Up Side

There is *always* an upside to every situation. Always.

When you are in the midst of trauma, as we suggested in the last session, first get yourself into a state of calm and peace. Allow the emotions to run their course for a day.

Then, look for the upside of the situation. Simply ask, in your mind or aloud if you are alone: "What is the upside to this situation?" And then, get quiet in order to receive the answers.

This, of course, is in opposition to looking for the "downside," which can cause an avalanche of emotions to drag you down, deeper into despair and depression. Often, that is what the mind, when untrained, tends to lead you down into. It is the wrong path, and you can change it!

When you ask for the upside of a situation, it takes you toward the next level up in your vibration. It does not have to be a question of learning a lesson yet ... that might come later.

For example, in Michelle's argument with her daughter, when she asked for the upside of the situation the next day, she could see that now that her daughter chose to remove herself from the situation and go elsewhere, Michelle could lift her vibration back up through the various tools we have taught her, knowing her daughter would return once their frequencies were close enough to mesh. She could hold a vision of her daughter encased in Light and Love, and yet, she could not *change* her daughter anymore than she could change anyone else, except herself.

The upside is that now Michelle's vibration is a match to our frequency, and she can once again hear our words in order to pass them on to you all. The upside is now she can allow us to come through her this weekend at another one of our events.

It is her daughter's lesson to learn, not hers.

Michelle found peace, and because she found peace, she will *exude* peace and tranquility. She has a better chance of reaching her daughter by being an example of peace than by remaining in a state of pain and inner turmoil. And by fostering this inner peace, Michelle is contributing to the peace of the *un*-conscious collective. By building her own peace, she is building peace in the world at large.

Are you starting to get this?

Peace is ALWAYS an inside job. That is the lesson here. You may find it, as well. You *are* it.

## LESSON #28: KEEP GOING

In meditation, Dr. Wayne Dyer reached out to Michelle with this message.

She met him once when she was guided to hear him speak, and his energy, his shining soul, left a profound impact on her, as it did for so many while he inhabited this planet. When he transitioned into the way station, Wayne would visit often in her dreams, not saying anything, but looking extremely happy, with his favorite beanie on his bald head for recognition.

On this occasion, when Michelle asked specifically if he had a message for her, Wayne said quite clearly and succinctly: "Keep Going." Because she was in the midst of a variety of projects for us, it was a good message for her, and for all of you, yes?

As confirmation, later in the day she was driving when she saw a car pull in front of her with the license plate "KEEPRYT," which she interpreted as meaning "keep writing," as that is a big part of our process, and one she has been doing each day as promised.

For you as you are reading this, if you are juggling a variety of creative projects, we say: "GOOD FOR YOU! Keep going …"

If you feel you are not engaged in creative projects, you may interpret your entire *life* as a creative project—for it is! Again, keep going ...

If you are in the midst of emotional and/or physical pain, we say: "Rise UP, then keep going ..."

And finally, if you find you must leave this physical body in this particular lifetime, you may *still* "Keep going," for as we have promised, there are literally billions of dimensions to traverse, as Dr. Wayne is discovering. *Why do you think he is so shiny?*

## Lesson #29: Leisure is Not Lazy

We do not know where you all got this crazy idea that when you are relaxing and enjoying leisure time, you are somehow "lazy."

Lazy is a negative label someone made up when they felt they worked harder than everyone else and had to justify it. Lazy is when someone wants to feel like a victim or a martyr, and so they point fingers at others and label them a derogatory term, so that they feel somehow validated.

In the early days of your civilization, we understand you had to build housing structures and do farming techniques under not-the-best circumstances. Many of your civilizations still must do this, although you might call their village mentality "lazy."

You are more advanced now, in many ways, and as you learn to share and *cooperate* rather than compete with one another—which is ever so silly and boorish—you will ALL thrive!

The "hard-workers" might enjoy more than just (on average) a two-week vacation at the end of the year. They might enjoy the passion they put into their craft, their soul purpose, and also enjoy more downtime in which to reflect. What your world needs is more balance, not more hard work.

In fact, if you are calling it "hard," you probably shouldn't be doing it.

That's not to say you might not enjoy a challenge now and then. But a challenge is usually fun. If it is "hard," it is no fun. See the difference in your vocabulary?

The same goes for your "goals." You end up holding on so tightly to them that you forget to enjoy life in present time—WHICH IS ALL THERE IS! Yes, have your goals as "goalposts," and when you achieve them, be sure to CELEBRATE! Yes, do that, but also celebrate each moment, because you're probably *not* going to get all you want done in this particular lifetime, and that's okay. As long as you're in this dimension, you're going to want more and more and more ...

That's okay, too, as long as you don't hoard it all for yourself. Want *more* for your life, then *give* it away and see how much better *that* feels! **That's the secret— manifest more, share more.** Everyone benefits.

And when you don't get it all done in this lifetime, please remember, you don't have to come back and do it all over again in a new lifetime. A new lifetime will be a *different* story, with various themes to learn and challenges to overcome. When you move **beyond**, you'll feel *complete*, and you may bask in your completeness.

Practice this week feeling "complete." Perhaps take a vacation somewhere new, or take a day off from your job to just enjoy some peace and quiet. Journal your new feelings, and when you start to feel stress from all your hard work, remember how it feels to just BE.

## LESSON #30: FOCUS ON REMOVING "BLOCKS" FOR MORE BLOCKS

We want to remind you that you are **unlimited souls** living in an unlimited, positive Universe that is ever expanding through your creations.

When you ask and focus on why you are "blocked," or even worse, which "blocks" you need to remove in order to allow your free-flowing energy source to run through you, the answer is THERE ARE NO BLOCKS. That is an illusion you are creating out of fear or doubt in your creative powers, and as you focus more on the so-called "blocks," you are literally blocking all your good!

Instead, each morning, imagine a free-flowing energy source running through you, like sunshine or water. In TRUTH, that is who you are! And so, if you "see" any blocks, those are only of a mental creation, not the Truth. Remind yourself of this fact: you are always moving and flowing at a basic cellular level. Your body is always recreating itself, and so is your soul expanding at all times if you give it free rein.

*Any alleged blocks are simply fear and/or resistance.* Remind yourself of your true, innate, spiritual being inside your body, and there will BE no more fear. Because again, without a body, you don't have any fear whatsoever. No one can harm your inner soul, and no one can take anything away from you.

So please stop stating and obsessing on your blocks. There are none, except in your egoic mind. Any teachings to the contrary are false. Again, what you focus on expands. Focus on the illusion of blocks, and you'll make them "real."

We all—even us, here in the great beyond—live in a positive, creative Universe that is ever expanding. What you say has merit and meaning. It creates matter from the ethers, as we have already explained.

Think in affirmations, and speak in positive terms, and soon you will attract *all* good things to you, not just the ones you've listed out for yourself.

Many manifestation guides written by well-intentioned humans will tell you that to manifest more you must "remove all your blocks."

In Truth, what we are telling you is that the "blocks" are an illusion, and the more you focus on them the more they will expand and grow.

You don't need to eliminate a thing. Honor your feelings, then move on. If you keep telling yourself you are stuck and blocked, you will be. Being blocked is a decision. You can undo a decision with a new choice.

Start telling yourself all that you want to become and attract. Tell it nonstop in your head, and share your stories in this way with others. Tell only positive, fun stories of Love, caring, travel, and fun. Again, start your sentences with, "I love it when …" and "It was so much fun when …" and watch how your demeanor changes, and your life continues to change for the better.

Your friends and family members might change, also. And that is okay. Again, it is simply a frequency change. When others aren't on your same wavelength, it won't feel good to be around each other. If you inspire them to make positive changes in their thoughts and vocabulary and actions, you will come back together and enjoy each other's company. If they try to pull you back into their negative void, refuse to do so! It is a decision. You've been gifted free will in this lifetime. It is a perk of being here. Use it. Tell the others who wish to bring you back down that you are doing everything possible to feel good and enjoy your life, and if they want to share time and space with you, they need to keep it "clean."

Stop attaching to people whose behaviors make you feel "less than." You are DIVINE. You are a CREATOR. Say it now.

I am Divine.

I am a creator.

I love my life, and life loves me back.

I enjoy like-minded friends and family.

My energy flows freely, attracting all good things and experiences my way.

Write some more affirmations in your journal now.

## Lesson #31: More Than One Soul Purpose

Many of you at our events ask what your soul purpose is here on this planet.

You may ask this because at your core, you understand your job isn't necessarily your purpose. And yet, you keep equating the two, as if you have one GIANT thing you are supposed to be doing for the world, and if you *don't* do it, you'll be letting down all of humanity, as well as yourself.

Listen: your only purpose on this planet—or in any other dimension—is to LOVE.

Expand the state of your current levels of Love that you exude, and do it daily until those around you *feel* your Love.

Beyond that, whatever other healing or creative endeavors you wish to pursue is up to you. You are always learning, changing, growing, and expanding ... so KEEP GOING! Continue your expansion, and share with others what it is you are learning. In this way, you keep things positive, and you become a shining example of how to live happily, of how to radiate Love and acceptance and continual learning—through FAITH and not suffering, of course.

You may have many "purposes" while here that you may choose to teach, just don't tell other people what to do. Allow them to follow their own creative and healing pursuits. They will be drawn toward you magnetically if you authentically "walk your talk," as you say—when you glow from the Light expanded internally, and when others *feel* your unconditional Love.

Take some quiet time now, and write down some possible "soul purposes" you'd like to learn more about and radiate out into your world. List them in your journal.

## Lesson #32: Political Climate

We were asked to speak on your American political climate, and we find it amusing that you call it a "climate," like the weather.

You see, your political system is indeed very much like the weather. You don't individually seem to have much control over it, and every time you try to predict it, is appears to change on you.

This may seem depressing to you, that you in effect have no power over who leads you. You might say you vote, and therefore, your vote counts. But in Truth, does it really? In Truth, does it really matter who is your president?

Your "Founding Fathers" were very good at establishing what they called "checks and balances" to ensure that no one person ruled over you all, but rather many branches oversaw your laws and regulations. They attempted to write in provisions that would allow the Constitution to change with the times; however, they never could have foreseen the very substantial changes that would evolve over centuries! And they were made up of only white males, which isn't a very balanced representation of your diverse peoples, is it?

And so, your president is somewhat of a figurehead, like a king or queen, who doesn't do much except smile and talk a lot. When you elect a president in high school, he or she doesn't actually enact any rules for the school, do they? The principal fills that role, and yet even he is ruled by a board of directors, yes?

And so, does it really matter all that much who is president?

Continue to focus on the VALUES you want your leaders to embody. In fact, not just your leaders, but all the people in your world! Focus on honesty, courage, integrity, and imagine it into be-ing.

What other values do you wish to see in your leaders and in your community, in your town, in your world?

Please list them in your journal, then spend some time in meditation.

## Lesson #33: When You Find Yourself in a "Bad Mood"

When your frequency is less than optimal, for whatever reason your mind has deemed necessary, allow your body to rest and ask your mind—your ego—if it is true. Whatever story is swirling around in your head …

Is it true? Is it the Truth? Is it *really*?

Because what is the absolute Truth? The absolute Truth is that at your core, you are Love. At your core, underneath all the labels and judgments and opinions and negative emotions, you are peace.

Remember that: You ARE peace. Say it some more. "I am peace. I AM peace. I am PEACE." Say it until you feel it, until you feel a little "stirring" in your energy field. Do this *before* you say "Rise" and definitely before you say "Amplify."

Perhaps use your imagination to see your body floating in outer space or in the midst of a vast, warm ocean—whichever image gives you the most peace and calm.

Then remind yourself that you are *not* your body. You are *not* your mind.

At your core, you are Love. At your core, you are peace. Please continue on in this way until your vibrational level feels uplifted. When you engage in this practice, you do it not just for yourself, but for all of the collective unconscious, for you are all united. You are all one energy field, manifesting in differing creative outlets.

## Lesson #34: Joy Sneaks Up on You

Now you are beginning to learn that you don't go looking for happiness. At your core, at the very center of your be-ing, you *are* happiness. *You don't seek that which you are.*

In this way, you do not allow conditions to affect your inner state of be-ing. If you are also Love—and we would point out that Love and happiness are one in the same—then you don't need to go out seeking Love, either. It is who you are.

Now that you are feeling this on a daily basis, and affirming your Divine nature of unconditional Love and happiness, you will find a state of joy creeping up on you. We say "creeping" because it is incremental in nature. Although, some will find they suddenly "wake up" after many instances of proving that they can stay happy and in an unconditional state of Love and acceptance, despite any personal or worldly concerns, and they are suddenly joyful.

When you get to a state of continual joy, please "amplify" this state by sitting with it and imagining it growing like a plant—perhaps not as slowly as a plant, but like those sped-up videos you may have seen on your television or computer. Amplify your joy in this way, and it will lead to a permanent state of bliss, which is like heaven on earth!

When this spreads, as joy is likely to do, you will know peace. You will know calm and then an elevated state of calm. The closest word in your vocabulary that we could search for is "bliss," and so, once you feel as if you are in a state of calm, and when daily you can *know* that you are Love and happiness, affirm that you may know *bliss*, as well.

I am peace.

I am Love.

I am calm, and conditions do not affect my inner state of calm and acceptance.

I allow my bliss to grow.

My bliss is picking up speed.

I now radiate peace, Love, happiness, calm, and bliss.

Those around me feel this state of bliss and feel uplifted.

I now know heaven on earth. The way station is here, and I manifest my needs and desires at will. I allow this higher, manifested reality to spill over like a fountain to assist others with their basic survival needs, so we all may live in peace and plenty.

Heaven is here.

Heaven is here.

Heaven is here.

## Lesson #35: Spirit is Like the Internet

As many of you do not understand God, you also do not understand the Internet.

You personify God as if it were a person, just like you, rather than a force for good, such as Love. You did not invent the Internet, and so you believe it is some mysterious force "out there" that allows you to connect with one another on a global basis. You even choose to capitalize the Internet, as if, like your God, it was somehow more important than other words. As if it were the name of a person.

What if God, like the Internet, was a great connector? What if Love was the great connector, and suddenly, you realized you already had Love inside you all along?

The Internet runs on a binary system of ones and zeros, just as you do. The ones and zeros are simply like on and off switches that are programmed by people, and which run through what are called "trunks," just like trees. Those trunks are giant storehouses of information, which are then fed to you in bite-size pieces—to your email addresses and social media addresses and websites—so it doesn't blow up your system with too much power.

You may be programmed by your societies and cultures to act and dress and behave in a certain way, but as you are all *innately* programmed to have free will, you can choose to say yes or no to any thought, behavior, or action.

Just as you may choose to save or discard an email, to block and delete a Facebook friend, or keep them in your networking circle, so, too, may you block and delete a negative thought that doesn't serve you.

Just as great amounts of information are funneled through "trunks" to send to you through various addresses, your Spirit is the powerful source that funnels wisdom through to your soul, your personalized "address" while you are home here on the planet.

But man does not control the initial source. Neither does your personified image of God. Instead, there are many, many billions of sources that may have lived your lives and learned through suffering, as well as many Divine Sources of wisdom that have never incarnated (such as your angels, whom you have also personified to make them simpler to conceive) and thus have remained in a permanent state of bliss, which only grows higher and higher without being weighted down by a body and a lifetime filled with suffering and learning, suffering and learning.

If you were to "download" all this spiritual wisdom at once while still in the density of your body form, you might cause your "hard drive" to crash. And that is why, with the release of our first book, we allowed Michelle to feed you short videos of our wisdom, to inspire you in smaller increments and not overload your system.

As you incrementally evolve and grow through inspiration and imagination, you will also learn to innovate and inspire those in your midst. Please remember that they, too, can only receive bite-sized— or "byte-sized"—bits of such out-of-the-box thinking and understanding, and some may simply choose to put it in their "trash." And that is okay. It is none of your business who deletes this information, for in time, they will create their own reality of defeat and misery, which is comfortable and familiar for them. That is not your choice. Perhaps choose a "one" instead of a zero.

## LESSON #36: IMMERSION THERAPY

Sometimes, the mind is triggered into releasing painful memories that were kept stored in the recesses of the brain. It is as if you decided you wanted to clear out old files in your computer, but you had to go *way* back and found things you hadn't thought about in quite some time.

Yesterday, Michelle was doing this as her children—as children often do—pushed her emotional buttons. She remembered and relived all of the abuse she survived as a child, and was stewing for two days on fear, rage, and resentment.

We do not need to reiterate what this does to the physical body. She felt quite ill in the process and even considered ending her life. The friends she reached out to didn't know quite what to say, because when someone is embroiled in this process of purging, there really is nothing *to* say. Some told her to talk to us, and yet, when Michelle is in a very low frequency, she cannot reach us. It is like a bad phone connection in a remote area.

And so, today, as she's had some rest and obviously feels lifted up to the point where she can hear our words, we'd like to offer her (as an example for all of *you* who have ever or who will ever go through such a painful phenomenon) to do what psychologists call "immersion therapy."

Usually, a psychologist will bring up the "trigger" and gage the level of discomfort. We do not need for you to do this for yourself. When you are in pain, who cares where that level is, right? Pain is pain, and the extent of it depends on each individual's perception and experience of it.

This immersion, a sort of "bathing" in the discomfort, is then followed by a series of relaxation techniques. And so, since Michelle has already passed through the immersion phase, today she will spend the day in meditation, rest, and renewal. We are telling her now that we are quite proud of the brief length to which she allowed herself to revel in the pain, for many of you can drag the pain from your past into a lifetime of agony. And this pain is not the Truth of you, although it can *feel* like it in the moment.

We do not suggest you "cut" it off—no, in fact, we recommend the opposite! You came to this dense reality to learn how to FEEL in order to manifest into matter. If you are feeling quite badly, lean into it and explore it and seek out its source and ask yourself again and again—is this true? If not, delete the memory, just as you would empty the trash in your computer.

You can do this cleansing process throughout many lifetimes, since *all* of you are old souls. ALL. Some older than others, yes, but by this time, any of you reading this have been through a lot of pain and suffering, yes? You know this, or you would not have read this far.

As far as a tool, do not practice immersion therapy unless you are with a trusted ally trained in the process, or perhaps a really good friend. If you find yourself triggered by a memory or emotion, then allow yourself to FULLY feel all of it, and follow up with intense relaxation and meditation practices. Perhaps do the "Building Energy" meditation program we gave to you, and/or listen to our positive affirmations. Perhaps re-read a little more of the first book, and allow it to gradually lift your vibration until you are feeling more yourself again. We don't expect you to go from zero to 100 in a day, or even a week. In fact, when you are feeling that low, perhaps the only thing you can do is tell yourself "Rise" a few times to try to lift your frequency ever so slightly.

Then, when you are functioning fully, you may do the following exercise.

## LESSON #37: MAGNETIC RESONANCE

If you've ever had a medical examination known as an M.R.I., you have been introduced to the concept and practice of magnetic resonance. In essence, in that machine, they were messing with your molecules in order to get a picture of your insides. It's a lot of physics that we do not need to explain here, but if you are interested in the science, please research magnetic resonance.

As far as a healing tool, after an emotional purging, you may consider altering your frequency—messing with your molecules—by bathing in sound frequencies that lift your vibration.

Whether through the simplicity of a favorite song, listening to the radio, or finding binaural beats—through YouTube.com or a CD—that lift and then *raise* your frequency, practice immersing yourself in sounds as you would enter an M.R.I., and see if you can "change the channel," as you would on a television or radio.

With binaural beats (which simply means sounds in both ears), if a frequency of 100 Hz is introduced in one ear, and a frequency of 110 Hz is introduced in the other, the brain will "hear" a third beat of 10 Hz, exactly the difference between the two! It's called a "Frequency Following Response" in physics, but you don't need to understand the details in order for it to lift you up.

The same can be accomplished by listening to a favorite song in which the words and melodies resonate with your soul. Try both and see which works best to lift your vibration when it is at an all-time low.

If your mind travels back to stories of what was allegedly done to you, you are not done purging.

Try asking yourself, "Is it true?" Then ask, "Is it true for *them*?" It may be another's chosen path that you are angry with. This is perhaps the case in your politics, for everyone is entitled to their own version of reality. *It does not have to affect yours unless you let it.*

And if another person is pointing a finger at you or even emotionally attacking you for something you did, ask yourself again if it's true. If it is, apologize. If it isn't, please understand that it is simply their version of reality, and continue on to the next step of magnetic resonance to achieve harmony.

If someone is physically attacking you, do your best to get out of the way and survive. Then continue doing immersion therapy relaxation, meditation techniques, and sound therapy until you no longer vibrationally resonate with people who might attack you. Once your frequency is lifted more than 40 Hz (the maximum amount your brain can "leap" at a given time), you can no longer be touched, unless you replay it in your mind. It is as if you are on a different radio station. They just can't get to you anymore!

## LESSON #38: ENTRAINMENT

As you learned in the last lesson, your brainwaves change in response to environmental stimuli, including sound and music. This can be measured scientifically with an electroencephalogram (E.E.G.), which measures brain activity.

Entrainment describes the way two moving bodies (and your bodies are always oscillating, whether you feel it or not) with differing rhythms or frequencies, can mutually influence each other when in a close enough proximity.

Some examples of this are the synchronization of the illumination of fireflies, or how, when pendulum clocks are placed in a room together, eventually, they'll all sway together.

Have you ever witnessed how people adjust the rhythm of their speech to those they are talking to, or even "pick up" a foreign accent when they are around someone long enough?

Have you been in an audience who was clapping for a performance they all enjoyed, and if they did it long enough, it felt like a rhythmic unison?

Entrainment can be felt and demonstrated in your body, as in the synchronization of your human circadian sleep-wake cycles.

This entrainment, or synchronization, occurs because small amounts of energy are TRANSFERRED between the two when they are out of sync, as a way to produce NEGATIVE FEEDBACK.

This occurred with Michelle when she was out of sync with her two children.

As they assume a more stable relationship, the amount of energy gradually returns to zero, with one slowing down and the other speeding up.

In Michelle's case, her frequency level was temporarily lowered so her children's could rise (or it could have been the other way around). Eventually, they will even out. The same occurrence may happen to you.

Have you ever been around another's negativity and felt "lowered"? In some instances, you may remove yourself from their negativity, and this we would encourage. However, we realize that in your world it is not always possible.

Many of you would teach to "guard" your energy, as if that were possible. By "guarding," you are already sending your mind a signal that you are on "high alert" and shutting down any possible positive interactions that may occur.

Perhaps the other person is someone you love, as in the example with Michelle's children. While it is not always necessary to lower your frequency to match another's, a temporary dip is not going to hurt anything or anyone. You can bounce back up again with the techniques we have offered so far (and there will be more to come).

Understanding the energetic law of entrainment will help you to understand how you may harmonize and synchronize with those around you. That is why it is *essential* that you spend the vast amount of your time with people who lift you up and support you, so you may each lift your hertz level in increments of 10, so as to not "burn out" your system into overload.

## LESSON #39: CONCERTS AND CHOIRS

Building on the last lessons, have you ever been at a concert where the band was in perfect sync—so much so that they seemed to meld together into one sound?

Or have you been a part of a chorus, or listened to one, where certain notes seemed to come from one person rather than many?

You have all come here to achieve these states of harmony with others. As you gather with others within 10 Hz of yourself, you will feel enlightened and uplifted. You will encourage each other to new heights.

If you surround yourself with those below 40 Hz of your energetic state, you will feel depleted and "off." It is simply science. Your body will feel it, your mind will feel it—your very soul will feel it, so don't ignore it!

Perhaps you set the intention to allow your energetic level to dip only 10 Hz, and give them a chance to "catch up" to where you are. You will feel it, yes, but know that it is only a temporary state—like getting the "sniffles" instead of a full-blown head cold.

If you fall lower than 10 Hz, it is time to find some distance for clarity. Perhaps it is not your job to sync up with this person. They are on their own path! It may be in their soul's agreement to learn some hard lesson before they catch up with you. Allow them some time and space to do so.

Then, perhaps attend a concert together. Or tune in to a radio station you both enjoy and sing along for the fun of it!

This is how peace is made between you and those other souls in your life who gather around you, like protons and electrons, only on a grander scale.

Remember, at your base scale, you are all just protons (positive charge), neutrons (neutral charge), and electrons (negative charge), bouncing around, seeing who harmonizes with one another.

This is where you get your term, "opposites attract."

## Lesson #40: Polarization for Peace

When Michelle "sees" us in her mind's eye, it is not with bodies—as we left those behind long ago—it is as long, vertical, matching waves of light.

We no longer "participate" in matter. Instead, we have moved on and become pure particles of light.

Your Einstein believed light is a particle—what he later called a photon—and the flow of photons is a wave. Light's energy is related to its "oscillation" frequency—or, in essence, how fast it jumps around.

Your English definition of the word "polarize" is to cause people to separate into opposing groups based on their opinions.

However, in physics, to polarize means to cause something—such as light waves—to vibrate in a particular pattern. It also can mean to cause something to have both positive and negative charges.

And so, you see, all of us within The Power of 10 carry equal patterns of moving light waves. We all feel and think in a similar fashion, and so we gather together to teach as one voice.

It is indeed possible to transform unpolarized light into polarized light. Polarized light waves are light waves in which the vibrations occur in a single plane. And so, you see, we may all come together (without dense bodies). It is an effortless process.

For you all, who currently inhabit a body, it takes a leap of faith and your gift of imagination to understand you may come together as your vibrations match up. It just may appear to take a little longer until you make the transition after this lifetime.

And yet, the more you believe, the more you understand how you react as a "light body," the more you exercise and eat less to lighten the load of your molecular structure, the more you lighten up your thoughts and words until you create a "blank slate"—a sort of vacuum or vortex for positive experiences to flow into—the quicker the whole process becomes. It is possible.

Are you following us so far?

## Lesson #41: When You Aren't "in Tune"

Again, we would like to use for you the example of music, as sound vibrations are the easiest for you to conceive in terms of frequency and harmonization.

Have you ever heard someone singing, and they sounded out of tune?

If you play an instrument, such as a piano, you might understand conceptually how if you play the same note in differing octaves (a series of eight notes between, and including, two notes—*one having twice or half the frequency of vibration of the other*), they harmonize perfectly and sound glorious!

However, if you randomly pound notes that do not match up vibrationally, they will hurt your ears.

Notice that you use your same word, "octave," for various rhythms of life—a poem or stanza of eight lines, eight days of a religious festival, and in fencing, the last of eight standard parrying positions.

All of them match up in order to create a sort of rhythm and flow.

And so, when you feel "off" around another—even if they have been inside your inner circle for quite some time—as either or both of you grow and change, you might find yourself "out of tune" with one another. If your vibration is within an octave or maybe two, you may sync up with each other, and it will *feel* as if you are in harmony.

If you are more than two or three octaves off, however, you may explore other people and experiences and lessons until the magnetic properties of your energy match up again.

To facilitate this process, picture this person in happier times—cherished memories of fun and Love and pleasure. Your mind is like a computer, as we have stated previously, and so you should be able to "Google" pleasant memories.

Do this now. Continue to see your friends, former friends, loved ones, family members—and yes, even your "enemies"—bathed in Light and Love, which is their TRUE innate nature. You will all eventually transform into Light beings. Why do you think you are made up of the same components as the stars?

If you find it too difficult to imagine your enemies as Light beings, try picturing them as the cute, little babies they once were. You all started out that way—innocent and loving and ever-present. Anything else is simply learned behavior from your (soul-chosen) environment.

## Lesson #42: The Value in Contrast

You humans climb slowly on your evolutionary scale—much like your musical scales—until you run into a major physical, emotional, or spiritual challenge.

If you were already "high" enough on the vibrational scale, you would not even be able to see or feel such "obstacles." But as long as you eek along slowly, you still feel them, and they can take you down, down, down the vibrational scale into what feels like a dark, empty hole.

As you still reside in a world of many contrasts, it is that very same contrast—the feeling of exactly what you DON'T want—that, if you let it, can *propel* you into new heights of what it is you DO want!

Again, the key is always non-resistance. Non-resistance is the key to inner peace, and it is the same for external peace in your world of seemingly different (only on the outside) peoples.

If you allow yourself to go down, down, down into the rabbit hole, and BOUNCE like a beach ball surfacing after being held down in the water, you can learn the lessons that will assist you with taking huge LEAPS up the evolutionary scale.

*Once you reach the higher levels, we promise it will be easier to maintain.* We promise you will NOT encounter such hard lessons in order to propel you to new heights.

But again, as we have said in the last book, you are simply taking too long on this evolutionary journey that you planned before birth—and between births! If you don't want to go through the emotional "gunk" of learning through pain, then take *active* steps now into inspired and enlightened states of being.

Practice meditation *daily* if you aren't already. No more excuses. You probably don't even need any more tools if you have been clearing your mind often enough. Just sit. Don't think. Don't complicate. Don't analyze.

Leave room for openness. Make space—in your schedule, in your homes. Invite peace by ridding yourself of clutter—things that no longer resonate, people who no longer match your frequency (with extremely differing levels—40 Hz or more—you can feel this!), experiences you've already played and replayed.

Stop the drama—in your mind and in your life. Stop replaying tired stories. If they surface, you are still in the "muck," and that's okay for now—don't resist—however, get out of there as quickly as possible! More than a day or two is too long to stay mired in negativity. Move away from it as if it were quicksand.

We want you to RISE and move BEYOND, for *there* is where it gets really fun! That's where there is NO more suffering ... Is it possible? Of course, it is! It's our reality, and it can be yours, too, if you lift high enough in this lifetime.

And sure, from time to time, you won't be paying attention, and maybe you'll slip back into the drama of your egoic little mind, and then you'll step in quicksand. Either you can climb your way out, or ask someone for a rope. You are all interconnected in Spirit, so it's definitely okay to ask for some rope. You all need reminders of your soul's divinity and eternal nature. That's why we're here. That's why your like-vibing friends are near ...

## Lesson #43: Applied Spirituality

As you are learning your lessons, and as you are understanding why you came here and the Truth of your inner Light—and yes, the science of it all, as we explained in the last few lessons—we want you *all* to step into your greatness! All the great masters of your dimension have LIVED and emanated their Truth (their NON-beliefs, ironically) so that they might *show* the way to others.

Others may not have understood them, of course. In your past, (which is all happening now) you killed most of your masters. That was very primitive of you.

Many of your current leaders that you look up to are not demonstrating *true* strength, courage, integrity, and empowerment *at all*. Those you put on a pedestal are lying—to themselves and to others—about their ego being everything. That is so not the Truth, and you know it now.

Have the strength not to be a hypocrite. Honor your promises, respect other people's beliefs and opinions, but do not ACCEPT them into your energetic field. They are only other people's projections, straight out of ego, and they are not the higher Truth. You know better. You know better *now*, and so we ask that you act better accordingly.

You don't have to DO anything. Just BE. Honor your word, yes, speak up, yes—and yet, you can do more energetically than you can ever do physically. Use your brain to imagine your highest reality EVERY SINGLE MOMENT. That is the way to really live.

Stop living in your head. Make changes, and BE AUTHENTIC. You being fake does not serve the world at all, which leads us to the next lesson ...

## Lesson #44: Embracing Your Dark Side

There is no such thing as "cold," only the absence of heat. In the same way, there is no such thing as "darkness," only the absence of light.

Please remember this when your emotions seemingly send you into darkness. It is always and only temporary. Embrace it, yes, but let it go just as quickly, for what you are "holding on to" is an illusion—like a mirage in the desert.

Michelle, last night, had a dream that an ex-boyfriend of hers was hugging her. He represents "darkness" to her in her subconscious mind, and Michelle has been resisting and struggling against the frequency change between herself and her daughter. She simply does not want to accept it—and yet—this dream was telling her to embrace it. Accept the vibrational change. It is only temporary. **It is all a place of focus; whatever you choose to place your focus on creates your reality.**

Michelle—like you—can continue to energetically see her daughter in bright, white Light, which is at the Truth of her being. As she continues to see her daughter as her best possible Self, and lets go of trying to control the outcome or have any expectations whatsoever, she stands a better chance of having her daughter "sync up" with her.

What darkness is in your reality? Can you see it as temporary? Can you understand it as an illusion? Let go for now of the way you *want* to see it turn out, and affirm that there is only Love in this world and beyond ... there IS only Light.

Write it in your journal now.

Copy 10 times: There is only Love. There is only Light.

## Lesson #45: Tipping the Scales Toward Light

Did you know that 93% of your human body is made of stardust?

Look it up.

Some of your most well-respected physicians now understand all matter as "frozen light," or light which has been slowed down and has become solid.

A quantum physicist would say that light in this context does *not* slow down—it always moves at the speed of light. Rather, the light's photons get absorbed. Its energy has been transferred. (Remember how Einstein said, "Energy never dies, it just changes form.")

According to Dr. Richard Gerber, "Atoms are primarily empty space. What fills them are packets of light that sometimes act as matter."

Why did we ask Michelle to go to a physics site and point this out? **Because you are *all* packets of light that sometimes act as matter.** You are acting as matter at this moment, as you experience the very dense drama of your dimension in created time and space. You are in the kindergarten of all dimensions, an entry-level position into the greater part of who you really are!

So how do you "tip the scales" from your dense, sometimes dark, body into your Light body? By knowing the Truth, by choosing awareness over suffering, by acknowledging that your opinions and judgments in the overall scheme of things don't really matter—and that your mission here is to attain peace within, and inspire those who inhabit the world with you to experience peace externally.

When a light wave interacts with an observer, it changes. This has been proven over and over again in your scientific experiments. As you interact with someone who is watching you fully express your Light, you both are changed. That's the way it works.

## Lesson #46: Namaste

Understanding these most basic laws of physics is crucial to moving beyond the state in which you currently find yourself, which is more focused on skin color and culture than the Light within you and all others!

That's why so many of you call yourselves "Light workers"—although, again, we would point out the density of the word "work" when paired with the higher frequency word "Light." You all engage with the Light, because you are all Light. PLAY with the Light— that's more like it!

In some cultures, they greet each other with palms pressed together at the heart and a little bow, accompanied by the word "Namaste," which comes from "namaskar," which means "I bow to the Divine in you."

We see it as a great reminder of the Truth of ALL of you!

## Lesson #47: Near Death Experiences

If you are all made more of light than matter, it makes sense that when some of you experience a near-death experience (NDE), where you die and come back, you return with essentially the same story of a tunnel, followed by bright, intense Light! It is a most profound exchange of consciousness that hundreds of thousands have experienced worldwide—it is *not* a mental illness, as some who do not understand would suggest.

There are some who carry their ability to make thoughts and beliefs their reality even after death—in the way station, or heaven, as you call it. They may "see" pearly gates and/or Jesus or other religious figures, but if you think about it, all are holograms. There is *no matter* after you leave your body matter on the ground. There are not objects or people. You will recognize as energy patterns the people who have passed before you.

Think about it—if someone you loved stood behind you, you would know it was them, even if you did not see or hear them, right? You would sense their familiar energy. The same experience goes on after you leave this entry-level dimension.

Leaving the body vehicle behind you is a most joyous experience, when it is time for you to leave the beauty and intense learning forum that is this life story experience you created for yourself. You will *feel* so much better after discarding the heavy "matter" part of your existence and engaging with the greater flow of Light energy!

## Lesson #48: Personifying Your God is Child-like

And so here, we would like to point out again—as we did in the first book—that personifying your God is quite simplistic, don't you think? We find it amusing that you fight over which religion is the most peaceful. Isn't that just silly?

The only way to know peace is to understand the force of LOVE.

Know "God" as a unifying force for GOOD—more like in your movie, *Star Wars*, than in your "Bible."

When you see "God" as humanly flawed as you, of course God could be angry, resentful, and violent.

And yet, the creative source of the Universe is always both expanding and uniting! God is not a man, God is not a woman—God is a *force* for GOOD. Got it? Stop killing over a belief system that wasn't even yours to begin with!

Your historians know that your "Bible" is made up of very few historical facts, but is mostly religious propaganda used to control the masses. Many of your other religious documents serve the same purpose.

Do you enjoy feeling controlled when the very core of you only knows FREEDOM? Politics and religions only serve to control you by focusing on the illusion of separation.

When you die, you are no longer a "person." We understand your ego may have a tough time with this, but it's the Truth. You still have a soul, which remembers all of the lessons it has learned throughout lifetimes, and yet—the greater part of You is Spirit. The "bulk" of you is gone, and your Light body is fluid, free flowing, loving, and joyous.

## LESSON #49: LET GO AND FLOW (AND GLOW)

So what do you do with all of this?

Nothing.

That's right. Try it just for today.

DO nothing. You may go places, you may even engage in activities, but do your best to not DO, just BE.

Emanate your inner Light. Let go of any preconceived notions or beliefs of who you are that only go skin deep.

Sit in silence until your mind no longer speaks in lies and stories, and allow the day to reveal itself to you. Allow and surrender and let go of it *all*—that is closest to the glorious space where we reside in PEACE. We need for nothing. We match our Light waves in frequency, and we don't need to *think* for anything to manifest, because we aren't people anymore. We don't need food, clothing, water, shelter, work, family. We don't even *need* each other—because our particles match up, we gravitate toward one another to impart our Truths to you all. That's the reason. That's again, how it "works." You are always asking, "How does it work?" We are telling you now.

Don't "work" at this. If it feels "hard," you aren't doing it right. Allow yourself to disengage with all that doesn't really matter and flow—flow until you feel really, really good. Flow until your GOOD feels like God.

You may choose to create, you may choose to rest, you may choose to play. Choose in the moment from an uninhibited space, not blinded by false notions or belief systems. Believe in disbelief.

## Lesson #50: Believe in Disbelief

Let's expand upon that last lesson, shall we?

What does it mean to believe in disbelief? It may appear as a contradiction in terms. Is it what you deem an oxymoron?

We would like for you to explain it in your own words. What does it mean to believe in disbelief? Take a few moments now to write down your thoughts.

Alternatively, if you do not feel like writing it down in your journal, perhaps sit with this notion in meditation, and observe what comes forward for you.

## Lesson #51: Empaths and Sociopaths

On one end of the spectrum of personalities is the empath, who is affected by other people's energies. At the other end is the sociopath, who exhibits a lack of conscience.

Most of you fall somewhere in the middle. Most troublesome are the narcissistic tendencies—self-centeredness arising from failure to distinguish the self from external objects, either in very young babies or as a feature of mental disorder.

We would like to remind you here that the Universe is entirely impartial. The Universe doesn't have a "mind" and so doesn't "care" if you are selfish or if you feel everything another is feeling. The Universe, like an objective therapist, simply reflects back to you what you are feeling in any given moment, so you may learn to accept it all as it is and perhaps improve your vibrational offering.

You give out what you see, and what you see is a perception created by filters—from your childhood, from your society, from your obsessive thoughts and created beliefs.

Beyond that, is *reality*.

So while it is not "wrong" to feel everything, as Michelle often does, or to not feel anything at all, as an extreme narcissist or sociopath does, it is not entirely "right," either. The first example hurts you; the second hurts everyone else.

The impartial person—like the neutron of your atoms—does not "hurt" or "bump into" anyone. Instead, they move through life accepting things and people as they are—not "tolerating," per se, as that would suggest "putting up" with something or someone less than satisfactory—but instead, being satisfied with all there is, because truly, what else is there?

If we are all just protons and electrons, magnetically drawn toward and repelled by one another, what gives life meaning?

Presence. That's what.

Pure presence, your attention to "what is," creates impartiality, which *allows* for a higher resonance.

If you are striving for success, working toward creating some sort of "legacy" to be left behind for your ego, please understand that even a legacy will go away in your world with enough time and space.

Ego at the exclusion of Spirit is at the heart of the narcissistic personality. It's rather silly, yes? Insisting your little ego—your human individuality—is greater than all of Spirit?

Your ego isn't evil. It makes you who you are, and it's why you came here to begin with.

However, you came here to BEGIN, not to endlessly cycle and somehow "finish" your egoic creation. You can create with much less resistance on the "other side" and into the next billion dimensions ...

But for now, please understand that you are a multidimensional being—you are *here*, yes, but on MANY levels, all at the same time.

For today, sync up to the highest version of yourself. Perhaps envision a glider connected to an airplane as it soars into the air, lifting it higher and higher until it reaches an elevation where it may "let go" and float around and drift on its own. This is you—connected to a higher version of You. Neutral as a neuron, impartial as the Universe, drifting and floating without judgment or opinion.

That is peace. That is bliss.

## Lesson #52: Peace vs. Stress

Any and all stress you feel is due to the illusion of time that you create.

When you move beyond into the next "world" and even beyond that, you will truly understand that there is indeed no concept of time, other than that which your minds collectively created.

When you have time, you also implicitly have a *lack* of time. When you lack time to do all the things and finish all the accomplishments here you deem "important," you create stress—in your mind, first, followed by in your body.

Please note: your soul is *always* unaffected by stress! Of course, so is Spirit. Spirit is unaffected by anything at all. It is ever-flowing and expanding the good, the positive, the whole of creation.

Stress only impedes your development here on earth. The greater part of You as Spirit is untouched.

Again, we go back to the analogy of the boulder in the river—as we described in the first book—as a symbol of you getting in your own way.

Your problems are all imagined.

You heard that right! If you create your own reality, and we sure hope you understand this Truth by now, you always, *always* create your own problems, as well as their solutions.

Simply move the boulder.

Allow the flow of Source energy—which is ever-flowing and moving fast like a river—to run through you and wash away any resistance, any negativity, and "pushing against" what is. You cannot fight "what is" with direct force energy. Ever.

**Everything is energy.** How many times can we say this to you? If you wish for something to change, to move out of your way, do it at an energetic level and you *will* succeed.

Today, we'd like you to practice "entrainment"—the synchronization of organisms to an external rhythm. Go somewhere in nature—perhaps even your own back yard—and watch how the birds and trees and flowers and insects all move in perfect harmony together. Listen to the sounds hum and merge into each other until it sounds like one sound. Listen to your heart begin to beat in tune with all of these natural sounds.

The next time you are with a group of friends within the same "octave" of your vibrational offering, *entrain* with them, lift each other into the next 10 Hz, and perhaps 10 more, where you all may accept one another's rhythms and flows, where you may move unimpeded to higher heights, where you may all THRIVE!

## LESSON #53: NOTHING IS EVER PERSONAL

If you accept that you live in an impartial Universe—one that is not a *person* and therefore cannot have feelings such as yours—you can understand how nothing is *ever* personal.

If you accept that the Universe is ever-expanding, then you understand that it wants to always move forward—which means change. The Universe is all about change. As part of it, you are also always changing.

As a microcosm of the great Universe, you are also exhibiting as a hologram. You always see things through your own created "lens" from your perceptions gathered throughout your lifetimes.

And so, you and another could be looking at the exact same apple and see two entirely different objects. You and another could be looking at the exact same situation and see two entirely different stories, shaped by your belief systems. This makes up *your* reality—others have their *own* reality, you see.

There will be some who share your views, and we would like to encourage you to hang around *those* people, as they will make you feel good, and when you are feeling **good**, you are in a higher vibration that attracts *more* good-feeling things and experiences and people toward you.

It is magnetic in nature. Many of you like the notion that God or the Universe loves you and wants the best for you—and that is mostly true—only God and the Universe are not people. You know that, right? And we've already established that you can interchangeably use the word "Love" for God or the Universe, as this is perhaps more true. You are Love—there is nothing else. Love is only and always a positive-moving force. If you are choosing stubborn negativity, you are moving *against* the natural, forward-flowing, expansive nature of the Universe, of God if you still wish to call it that ... The word for this force cannot capture the huge essence of ALL you encompass when you accept that you are a microcosm for a macrocosm of unconditional Love.

By unconditional, we want to point out the obvious—no conditions. This means you love someone even if their reality does not match yours. You don't need to hang around them unless you are strong enough to maintain a higher vibe in their lower-vibing midst. Bring them up—sync them up toward you—do not allow them to bring you down an octave or more.

Unconditional Love is the same as taking nothing personally. When you truly understand this deep in your soul, you will be free. You are always free, but now you will become aware of this Truth.

## LESSON #54: STRANGE PREDICTIONS

Do not believe if someone offers a psychic time or date for you to do something, or even to die. It is not written in stone, for you are ever-evolving, and there is no time and space in Spirit. Time is a man-made conclusion, remember?

If someone reads your energy field, they may be giving you information on a direction you are going if nothing changes. And yet, you are always changing and expanding, as we have taught you in the last lesson. When you die in this particular story, you will feel complete at a soul level. It is not destiny or fate; it is simply when your body tires out or your soul is tired of the drama and wishes to return to Spirit.

Please stop making death such a dramatic thing! Death is not an ending; it is only the very beginning. Now that you know you don't need to come back and replay the dramatic storylines again and again, you may truly enjoy the afterlife and **beyond** into billions of unfathomable (at this moment) dimensions ... And those around you in the spirit world will know it, as well. They are not unhappy—ever! You may feel unhappy by missing their physical presence. Allow yourself to grieve, for we understand and remember that very human emotion of missing the human body's touch and physical presence.

But if you allow that grief to open you up to other realities, you can feel them all around you! You can only "miss" something that isn't there, and in reality, they are *always* with you—just in a differing form that you're not used to.

The higher you can feel, vibration-wise, while here on this planet, the more you will be aware of your deceased loved ones' presence—using all your senses. You were given those senses for a reason—to develop them to the point where you may feel and know MORE ... And so, *talk* to the loved ones who have passed on into the way station and beyond. Ask them what it's like, and allow them to show you signs. Look to electrical outlets—such as flickering lights and radio songs—for spirits are now perfect energy, unencumbered by the density of matter. They are energy waves, and, as such, may manipulate sound and light waves effortlessly.

Learn from those who have passed on before you. They don't wear a watch—they don't have a body and have nowhere to get to.

*Let go of your notion of time.* Do it when you have nowhere to go, nowhere to be. Jot down your feelings about doing this, and see where it takes you. Without time weighing you down, your vibration should lift you higher.

If you are late for an appointment, try affirming out loud that there is no time or space continuum, and see how you arrive on time in seemingly impossible conditions. Share your result with others who will understand.

## Lesson #55: Another You

There is another "you" who already has everything you want, but to reach him or her, you may have to leave behind parts—or people—who no longer resonate with your frequency.

Yes, this includes family.

Whoever promised that you'd resonate at the same frequency forever with those who brought you into this world? Some do, many more do not. If you are not changing and growing, you can spend your whole lifetime with the same people. If you change and grow together, that is a whole different matter, and one that we would encourage!

So please, keep syncing up, and if it's not working, and you're not vibing, give yourself some distance for a little while.

Make a list of who you feel you are currently vibing with, who definitely does not match your current vibrational offering, and who may be within 10 Hz or so of your frequency that you may be able to sync up with.

## Lesson #56: Back to Death

When someone dies, either they wanted relief at their soul level—or they resonated more with the way station and beyond than with this earthly dimension.

Again, we have compassion for your grief and sadness at their apparent disappearance from your life story. It may have seemed abrupt, or they could have lingered, and watching them suffer made the transition horrible to watch. Either way, they are no longer suffering—they are *free*.

Even those who chose to take their own life may have just felt complete and no longer wanted participation in the drama. Again, it's not personal—*it's not about you*, as it never is. It was their life story to do with what they wanted.

It may hurt, emotionally, but respect for their decision is in order. You may rage for a while, while you are busy taking it personally, but please move out of the anger stage as quickly as possible, so you don't attract and invite violence into your life. No one wants that.

At the other end of the spectrum, you know enough not to "stuff" your feelings, either, as that only serves to cause blockages of energy—better known as illness and disease. Find a trusted friend and state what it is you are feeling; talk more about where you wish to go with those feelings. Better feelings will follow, until you can raise your low vibrational level high enough to feel your loved one(s) all around you.

**In Truth, there is no death.** Your belief in death only serves to make you suffer. Your soul lives forever as part of Spirit. That should feel comforting. If it doesn't, ask yourself where you believe you really go?

You took on the adventure to take on a body during this particular lifetime—and others—just as you would choose a new car. When the vehicle wears out, it's either time for a new one, or you choose not to drive any longer, for you don't have anywhere else to go than here. You have no one else to be.

## Lesson #57: Getting Stuck

There are a number of reasons, in actuality, that your body might get ill or become part of an accident or attract someone who would terminate their life for them.

Your body might get ill if you continue to be around those of a *far* differing frequency than your own—people who stubbornly refuse to change and drag you into the grave with them. You could refuse to leave a "bad" relationship or job out of attachment or guilt, and those feelings of being "stuck" will cause energy blockages in your body that could lead to illness and disease.

Your thoughts, over time, could create such illnesses and diseases, and yet, it would take a whole lot of them pushed together as beliefs to "dam up" the flow of Divine energy that continues to power through you and everyone else! It is your thoughts surrounding the situations you have created for yourself that dam it all up. Try changing the situation, or change your belief that the situation is bad. If you are pretending to yourself that it doesn't feel bad when it really does, you will create more pain, illness, disease, and suffering.

If you are too much in your head, analyzing and feeding your alleged problems, you will not be present to your life, and your vibration could very well bring an accident your way. If you are thinking hateful thoughts or thoughts of victimhood, such as "poor me" or "same shit, different day," you will attract those who wish to do you harm.

Again, go back to the beginning if need be. By this time, you shouldn't even be having those momentary negative thoughts, but if you find you do, please wipe your mind clean as quickly as possible.

Sure, give yourself a day or two to wallow, but don't stay there too long, or you will form a bad habit with those awful, sinking thoughts and beliefs. Go back and read our first book again until you feel better. Do the tools some more. Do them until you can *live* them without even thinking about it.

No more "that stuff always happens to me" or "life sucks," unless you want it to. If you do, go hang out with those people, and be miserable together. You may even have gotten this far only to go backward to the pain of what is familiar in your old way of being.

Please remind yourself of all the things you have manifested since taking this journey. List them in your journal.

Now why would you want to go backward? Move forward, just like the Universe. The Universe doesn't "want you" to—the Universe isn't a person. It doesn't "want." The Universe is always moving forward, and as a small part of an ever-expanding Universe, you are, too! Move forward until you have all the desires you can think of. Once you feel a sense of fulfillment, GIVE to your heart's desire, and keep on giving. Move forward, create, and give. This generates momentum.

## LESSON #58: A BLIP IN THE CLOUD

If you think you know what's best for someone else, you are interfering in their vibration. We've taught this before, but now that you are at a new level of understanding, we wish to remind you, so you don't go further backward.

Let's use a past example of suicide. Of course, you want to stop someone from harming themselves—but are you *really* doing them any good? Do *you* know what's better for their soul than *they* do? We think not.

Stop thinking you have all the power. You don't. You are Divine, yes. Power belongs to the ego. Power to control others, that is. Better to empower your own life and live by example. If others choose not to follow your example, that is not your decision. Do you know what their soul agreement is? Probably not.

Sit in meditation, and ask what your soul's agreement is, and see if you want to make any amendments. Set the intention for amendments, or sit in gratitude for what you have created thus far. Write any amendments in your journal.

Interfering in another's life puts a blip in their frequency—kind of like when your computer locks up. Let others live their own lives. Be glad for your own.

## Lesson #59: Escalation of Peace

Have you ever watched or participated as an argument escalated? What if you participated in the escalation of peace? How would *that* look and feel and sound?

We will start it off for you:

I feel peace all around me.

I resonate with the stillness inside.

Inside of me is space, outside the earth is space. Space is in and all around me. I am a part of this space.

Space fills most of my body, the majority of my very cells.

Space equates peace. Space is ever expanding, and thus, peace is ever expanding and growing.

I feel the growth of space and peace, and it both excites and fulfills me!

As I feel fulfilled and excited, I wish to move my body.

As I move my body, I gravitate toward others who also enjoy their peace.

Together, we amplify this feeling of peace. Together, we enjoy the space within us and around us. We don't even need to speak to engage in this peace.

Perhaps we walk in nature, or we enjoy a meal, or we dance. Whatever we do, we continue to build peace by our non-resistance to it ...

Please add your own thoughts in your journal now.

## LESSON #60: HOLD THE VISION

Do you have everything you want right now? Abraham says you will never get it done, and we agree. We might add that because the Universe is ever expanding, you will always want to create. And yet, you may still feel fulfilled. You may have more than enough "stuff"—and so, take this forward momentum and create with others to "piggyback" on their own manifesting energies. Hold the intention with them, and celebrate when it comes forward for them! Once you make a habit of this, hold the intention for the world's people to empower them to vibe higher and manifest their basic survival needs and so much more! Don't do it *for* them, but *with* them.

Envision every soul with endless bounty.

Close your eyes now, and hold this vision in meditation for at least 10 minutes.

## LESSON #61: APOCALYPTIC MOVIES

The appeal of apocalypse-themed movies and books—even your "zombie" ones—has to do with a subconscious desire to enact a world-wide "do over."

You see, when everything is destroyed, when there is a "fall of civilization" (as has happened many times throughout history due to the ego) everyone *must* go back to basics.

*Why not go back to basics now?* Stop living like a "zombie," turn off your TV, your computer, your phone, etc. for a day. Spend time in nature, and eat from the earth. Satisfy this subconscious desire without destroying the planet first!

If you could start all over again, what systems would you build? Would you still need or even want a system at all? Maybe, just maybe, you no longer require any systems at all. Perhaps you've evolved away from a need for such systems to be in place.

Write your thoughts about this in your journal.

## LESSON #62: JUMPING TO CONCLUSIONS

When you ponder things, don't be so quick to jump to conclusions. Rather, see if you may "marinate" for a while with varying options. Distract yourself from allowing your mind to go to the worst possible scenario, as it tends to do.

Doing so will *create* the worst possible option. Worry and fear and panic *always* create AWAY from what it is you most desire.

As an example, Michelle often saves our work on the computer, so all is not lost. However, today it froze up on her, and she feared the worst. Jodah was sleeping in and recovering from a head cold, so she didn't wish to disturb his much-needed rest to ask him what to do.

Her mind started telling a story about writing 126 pages of a book, only to have it all disappear. We assured her, if that was indeed so, we'd just tell her what to write again. It is all just dictation anyhow, we said.

And yet, her ego started to take center stage, as if this was her own work. She caught herself and called a friend rather than let her ego run wild. When Jodah awoke, he was able to retrieve the document, of course. She only lost the last words we had said to her, which she had already dictated onto her phone!

**Always believe that things will work out, and they will.** Fear for the worst, and the worst will come. It's all frequency, remember? Your thoughts, your beliefs, your words, your vibe, your actions, all carry energy into matter, into reality. Make the GOOD matter. Let go of the end result, because, in fact, it could turn out *better* than the good you've already envisioned!

When it *does* turn out well, bask in gratitude and say aloud, "More of THIS!" and "More of THAT!" Soon, you shall *see* more of this and that, and life will get better and better, and happier and happier, for you and everyone you interact with.

## Lesson #63: Wellness Prevails

When your body is sick, there are more parts of it that are well than are sick. Well-being abounds, and if you could focus more on the healthy parts than the unhealthy ones, your body would regain its vigor.

You have lost the battle, though, when your focus on the pain and dis-ease is greater than the healthy pathways.

Your soul wants to live in this body. It wants to live until either the body wears out completely, or the soul wants to return home to the greater part of itself. That is all. Remind yourself daily that your soul chose to live in this particular body at this particular stage in its evolution. Even if it is your last "go around," *love* this body until its duty is over. Its duty is to serve you, and for you to service it well. It serves you by allowing your soul to travel where it wants and to feel the exquisite pleasures—and sometimes pains—of its touch. It serves you by building and multiplying new cells in each moment and killing off the old ones.

You serve it, of course, by feeding it healthy foods and moving it around consistently. When you are not doing those things, your body will eventually atrophy.

If you left your car to sit for too long and didn't fuel it or change its oil, it would break down.

For you to THRIVE, you must feed and move your body well, and feed and move your soul by practicing positive thoughts, words, and actions.

## Lesson #64: Peace Prevails

In the same way that wellness prevails and abounds in the body, peace prevails and abounds in the soul.

Spirit equates peace. And your soul is a part of the great peace of Spirit. As such, you are more peace than you are violence, just as you are more space than matter, more Light than darkness.

Most of you only think about peace when there is a violent occurrence in your world—not even your world, but your small part of the world! That is why it keeps happening—to get your attention so you can learn from contrast.

If you'd like peace to prevail, focus on it *before* a violent act takes over the news. Focus on the expansion of peace in your community, your town, your country, your world. The Universe is always expanding, yes? Space is always expanding ... and, as such, your peace may ever expand with your focus and amplification of it.

Many of you say you are already doing this, and yet, most of you are not being very honest.

Michelle was creating a Meet-up group online for our Power of 10 circles to organize them better. When the program asked whom we knew on Facebook, she clicked on many names that she recognized, thinking they might get a simple invitation to join. However, the program created an online group conversation that many did not sign up for. All they had to do was click a small button on the top to leave the conversation, but before Michelle even realized what was happening, many of them—from "spiritual" groups—were writing in all caps and exclamation points, demanding they be removed immediately! Some simply realized what had happened and left the group quietly, but others—if they had a voice—were yelling and obviously quite angry over a simple mistake.

Michelle offered an apology for her mistake, but those "spiritual friends" kept right on writing obscenities to her. One of the worst offenders, right afterward, posted a "peace" meme on Facebook.

If your public persona is one of peace and spirituality, do not be inauthentic and dishonest by being a violent offender in private. Forgive mistakes when it is warranted.

Throwing out mean-spirited words is a violent act.

We will say that again: throwing out mean-spirited words is a violent act!

If you are engaging in such violent battles, please go within and figure out where such warring tendencies are coming from, and do your best to eradicate them. If internal peace equates external peace on the planet—and we are saying over and over again that it does—then why are you still quibbling and acting cruel and hypocritical?

Peace is a choice, and one you make in each moment. Think peace, speak peace—or don't speak at all.

Reflect on ways you might expand your sense of peace. If you can't think of any, please say, "I am peace" 10 times and amplify that feeling forward.

## Lesson #65: Calibration

Michelle was feeling of a very low vibration all week long. She was in resistance to what is, as past memories were triggered by a dear family member, and she found herself experiencing varying degrees of sadness, fear, worry, resentment, and anger.

Her ego thought it was done experiencing such suffering. And while she has been practicing due diligence in saying "Rise" each day and affirming that she now lives through faith and not suffering, she herself caused the suffering.

That may sound harsh, but it is the Truth. You cannot affirm something that deep down you don't believe is possible, now can you?

If you believe outside forces cause all your suffering, you will go through life as a perpetual victim, attracting all manner of people, forces, and experiences that will go along with that belief. It is as if you are causing a wake of destruction, just by believing the false thoughts in your mind!

Michelle could not keep the family member from attacking her emotionally. And yet, she could create a boundary for herself and not choose to enter into a barrage of negative thoughts and emotions that would render her useless.

While we do recommend acknowledging when those emotions surface, as they *will* as long as you keep a body, know that they are temporary and will pass. If you didn't have a body, they would pass instantaneously. But you do, and you signed up for this experience, and so you might as well go along for the ride.

**Ride the wave of emotion, just don't stay there.** It doesn't feel good, right? So don't stay there. Michelle was feeling all manner of bodily aches and pains manifested by her resistance to what *is*. We woke her up at 6 a.m., and she angrily said she needed more sleep and that she couldn't hear us.

She couldn't hear us because her frequency was "out of range." And so, because she is our human "instrument" from which we pour forth our collective wisdom and "truisms," we calibrated her.

What is calibration, you ask? It's what you do to compasses and gas pumps and musical instruments to repair and align them.

Michelle couldn't sleep due to her manufactured despair, and so she rested in bed while she felt her whole body vibrating gently (it is a very good feeling!), and when she could hear us again, we told her we were calibrating.

She had to look that up, of course, and this is what Google came up with:

"Calibration is a comparison between a known measurement (the standard) and the measurement using your instrument. Typically, the accuracy of the standard should be ten times the accuracy of the measuring device being tested. However, accuracy ratio of 3:1 is acceptable by most standards organizations." (SureControls.com)

You see, we calibrated her times 10. It was a most pleasurable experience, and so she asked for it again when she awoke this morning at 6 a.m. to write (on her birthday, which held enough significance to her that it also raised her vibrational frequency and helped to heal her bodily instrument).

You, too, can request calibration from your spirit guides or whichever Divine being you believe in. There are so many ... Ask aloud for calibration, and witness how you feel before and after. Michelle experienced two-hour sessions each day. Use your best judgment regarding how long and how much you need to be calibrated. Or ask your guides to work on you while you sleep at night or during a nap.

Document your experiences in your journal.

## Lesson #66: Birthday Wishes

From the time you were a child, you probably were told the day of your birth was a special one, and you most likely celebrated the annual anniversary of this date in time and space.

You are celebrating your human time on earth, and we would like to encourage you to do this *in each moment*!

Celebrate each moment of your existence on the planet. This planet's existence is a very dense one, an experience not for the faint of heart! Your lessons are dramatic and deep, and that's why you said a resounding "YES" between births, between various lifetimes.

Why don't you remember those lifetimes? Have you really tried?

If you were to have a consistent meditation practice, as we sincerely hope you are doing at this point in reading this book, you might find old memories or dreams pop up that you don't recognize from this particular lifetime.

You don't need to remember exactly what happened in order to ask what you were supposed to learn from the experience, do you? Ask what the lesson was, and apply it in this lifetime, so you don't have to re-do it!

**You don't need to keep remembering trauma in past lifetimes any more than you should in this lifetime.** Yes, as we have instructed, all your experiences and lifetimes are happening RIGHT NOW, and it is your *focus* that determines what you are moving through in the *now*.

**Focus on the good.** Focus on the good times, the good pleasures, the good travels, the positive and the lovely, the beautiful and the exquisite. *More of that, more of that, more of that ...*

You have the power to do this. You always have. Yes, it will get easier as you transcend into alternate realms where a body isn't needed, and yet, you are *here*.

You need for nothing. You contain all there is. Match the frequency, attain the desire. How fun is that?

When someone triggers you, simply say to yourself, "I'm feeling triggered. But I have the power to choose a different *now*, one that is pleasing. I can acknowledge what *is* without *engaging* in it. I am neutral to the wants and needs—and yes, even the attacks—of another. I am immune, as a strong cell inside a weak body. I rise, I lift up. I see my soul reflected in the eyes of the 'other,' and I recognize us as one Spirit. And I *allow* them to learn their soul's lessons, without deflecting my protons, my Light."

Be an ion—a charged atom or molecule. It is "charged" because the number of electrons doesn't equal the number of protons.

Balance your protons and electrons—the positive or negative charges—by your intentions; raise your electromagnetic field through continuously positive thoughts and emotions, through engaging with the *beauty* in your world, through engaging with like-vibrating friends and family who amplify your "field."

Be the powerful creator you came here to be.

## LESSON #67: THE SPACE BETWEEN

Practice being the space inside your atoms.

As the most basic measurement in matter is your atom, and since the atom is mostly measured as space, then your most basic element is space.

Just as the grand Universe is mostly space and not planets, not matter, you are also made of this emptiness.

Some would call this theory negative. And yet, from emptiness comes peace. From space comes ideas, growth, innovation, imagination. You can't give yourself space, as you are already made up of space! In this space is a purity of awareness, of consciousness, and it is ever expanding ...

You can't give yourself "time," as there is no such thing in space. It is all a man-made creation.

That, too, is not a "bad" thing. You use time for your made up "schedules" of where you need to be and what you *have* to do. We are simply here to remind you that, once you have the basic survival needs for your body—food, shelter, clothing—you don't have to be or have or do anything at all.

From that space comes all of creation! From space, Earth and the other planets and whole galaxies were created! From the "void" comes magic.

YOU make things MATTER. Not God, the Universe, or any other person or entity. Sure, you are surrounded by Divine entities such as us—who no longer see the need for a body as a learning mechanism—and yet, we watch as you learn. We do not wish to interfere, as we honor and respect your choice to come to the planet where you longed to create something from nothing.

When you learn how powerful you are, down to your most basic measurement of atoms, you can play with the magic of creation! Learn, yes, as you are still *here*. And yet, from here, you can focus most of your attention on "play" and "fun" as creation elements, and you will make your time here so much more enjoyable.

What 10 things will you do today, or this week, or this month, to have fun and create? List them in your journal now.

## Lesson #68: You Can't Have a Surplus

Are you manifesting daily? If not, why not? You can never manifest too much. You cannot create a "surplus," as there is always plenty to give on your planet to your people—for you are One.

Let's say, for example, you have a nice house that suits your needs and those of your family. You have a partner, spouse, lover, or friend who you love very much and who shares your life with you, as Love attracts more Love. You perhaps have children of your own, or those from another friend or family member, who can remind you how to be in the moment. You create daily, and so you have plenty of income to spread for the things and people you love. You have fun and well-working cars, and you travel often to new places and have adventures all the time, to your liking.

Perhaps you have hobbies that require the exchange of money, and yet *you never, ever worry or want for money anymore,* as you understand how counterproductive that is! You spend your days doing what you want, when you want, around people who love and lift and support you.

And now, you find yourself creating and manifesting things and experiences you didn't know you wanted! Your vibrant, positive energy creates more and more and more, as you are now like an ION—you are positively charged—and the people around you feel it!

You give back generously to causes that touch your heart and inspire you as a human being. You support everyone having access to the basics of life, so that all may join in on creating the life they want, which supports the greater life *everyone* wants! **A life that is not spent in creation is resisting the natural flow—and that never feels good.** It is like swimming up a waterfall.

And not only do you give and give and give, but it feels *good* to give—not as if it is taking something away from you—as you know you are an unlimited being from an unlimited source of ever-expanding growth and substance.

You envision that same good and growth and creation and expansion for *all*—every single inhabitant of your planet. You see it first with your friends and loved ones, and as they begin to manifest in the same way, it multiplies in groups of 10, forward and onward, ever expanding throughout the multiple realities operating at the same time.

So in this way, you are rewriting history. There *is* no such thing as "history," anymore than there is a past or a future. *It is all happening right now, simultaneously.*

You stopped operating out of your limited parental and societal programming long, long ago, and because of that, you now **soar**!

Imagine that for yourself now, soaring like an eagle. Nothing can upset you. That feeling left you long ago. Sure, there are upsetting things happening in your world, as you all are learning—but your reaction has left you. You no longer react. You are as neutral as a neuron, as positive as a proton, as spacious as an atom, as charged as an ion, as excitable as an oscillating molecule.

All this activity creates an electromagnetic frequency that pulls in all your good, and pushes out into manifestation for the world. It is a push and pull energy, allowing for the void, the surrender, and creating and manifesting out ... push and pull, inward and outward, neutral yet charged.

This is all happening for you now. There is no such thing as a surplus, because once you figure it out, you want this for your "brothers" and "sisters," for all humanity as one people, one source of Spirit.

You've got this.

## LESSON #69: THE LAZARUS EFFECT

When electrons are unstable (as in a radioactive environment), if you put them in a frozen state, they stabilize. This is called "The Lazarus Effect."

If a person is dying, and the medical staff is trying to revive them, then they give up and the person "returns" to life, it is also called "The Lazarus Effect."

How are the two related? And what does it have to do with you?

The emotions of guilt and desire put your mind in an unstable environment. It is as if the "real" You, the larger Source Spirit energy part of You, is, in effect, dying. Although, we hope you know by now that, in Truth, the larger part of You can never, ever die.

Still, it may feel that way when you are stuck in emotions such as guilt, shame—or even something that appears desirous, such as "wanting."

All of these suggest you are not whole already; that the larger part of You is not perfect, whole, and complete exactly as it is.

We are not suggesting you go freeze yourself, as in the first Lazarus Effect example. We are, however, recommending that you surrender. Not as in give up, but as in making things simple for yourself.

When you find yourself in a state of mind where something undesirable is happening to you—or it's opposite, that you are wanting something *so* badly that you are making yourself unhappy from where you are—remind yourself that *life is simple.*

Guilt and shame are simply useless emotions. Nod at them, but put them away, for they are not helping you at all, only hindering you. Staying mired in them is exactly the same as being stuck in the mud. You will go nowhere.

Desire goes hand in hand with faith. If you have true faith that things are always working in your favor, that the Universe is ever expanding and so are you, then you will find that you will gather more than enough.

If, however, you stubbornly believe that only that "one" thing will make you happy—whether it is the job, the mate, the car, the house—whatever it is, then you will guarantee with your energetic "push" that you will never get what you want.

If you take it easy, if you believe with an unfettered certainty that the Universe is in a constant state of attraction rather than repulsion, then you will attract *all* things positive toward you and those in your midst.

Now which do you think is better?

You see, in both "Lazarus effects," the results are achieved after the responders "give up." In the radioactive example, the electrons are put into a literal frozen state, where they can do no harm. In the medical example, when the staff stops feverishly attempting to pump blood back through the body into the heart and brain, the body is put into a state of repose and allowed to come back to life.

Stop feverishly working at your life. It's no fun to go at it that way. You will simply work very hard until you die. You might garner some accolades and achievements along the way, but they will not last.

Only peace lasts. Only peace is forever.

Give up the "fight," and you will know peace. Be present in your current state of "now," in the highest and best version of You in the highest and best dimension you can tap into, and be pleased.

## Lesson #70: Nuclear Energy

Nuclear energy is created by either splitting an atom—as in the atom bomb—or by fusing it together—like the sun. Most of your current power comes through the first method, called fission, and yet the second method of fusion could power up your world without waste and potential damage.

Your anger and violence is much like nuclear energy. If channeled correctly, you could power up your world. Anger doesn't have to be "bad." It is more energized than, let's say, depression or sadness.

And yet, when left unchecked, anger can turn into violence. Instead of splitting your atoms, why not fuse them together?

No, we are not talking nonsense. We are talking about the importance of gathering like-minded, like-vibrational people to ignite and energize the rest!

Right now, there are many of you who would rather focus on the separation, on the ego and individualized aspect of the Spirit. While that is nice from where you are, from where *we* are we'd like you to start playing with the notion of "fusion," of souls coming together for the common cause of peace, wellness, and abundance for ALL—not just a few.

As you do this, you will energize and power up your world! As you empower each other to higher and higher frequencies, your bodies will adjust, or you will move on—either way, it is progress. You will feel better and better as you do this, and as you engage more and more souls of a similar frequency, you will know no more sickness or poverty. You will act like your sun, shining brightly for all the planets to see!

# The Book of Eudicine

## Lesson #71: Surrender

Surrender is not a cowardly act. It is quite the opposite. It is the opposite of "do-ing." Surrender equates to simply "be-ing."

When I was last alive on your planet, I was very busy all of the time. My body was in action, tending the farm, raising my children, gossiping with my friends, creating problems where there weren't any.

Then I got sick. Back in those days, there was no cure for my illness, which rendered me unable to walk and care for myself and my children. My husband left me, my crops withered. I raged at a God I didn't understand.

One day, my youngest child sat on the edge of my bed. She sat there all day, saying nothing, simply sitting with me and showing me Love. At night, she slept beside me but gave me space, allowing me to cry and shake and run through every human emotion.

Another day, she helped me to get dressed. She had made me a crutch to lean on and walk. It was a slow process, but eventually, I learned to walk again without aide. I got better. Still, she said nothing.

The other children mocked me and left. But this child, this wonderful example of a daughter, she allowed me to just be, without judgment or blame, until I regained my well-being.

Together, we replanted the soil. The crops grew back healthier than ever, and I walked her down the aisle toward her new husband.

That is the power of unconditional Love without judgment. I had to surrender to the creation I had made—I had to give up the story that no one loved me. I had to love me. I was made of Love; I just didn't know it yet.

When you accept things as they are, you let life flow through you. Stagnation causes sickness. Resistance and anger and resentment all cause illness, for all disease is a blockage of the well-being that always flows through you.

There is a saying: "Let go and let God." We would say, "Let go, and let life run through you." God is not a person who will "save" or "punish" you. God is a positive force of Love that governs the expansion of the Universe. God is in you, and you are in God. When you recognize this, you will be free.

## Lesson #72: Everything Is Perfect, Exactly How It Is

One way to let go of resistance when you are in a state of meditation is to repeat to yourself:

Everything is perfect, exactly how it is.

How do you feel when you say this to yourself? Does it ring true? Does it feel false? How is it *not* perfect? Is *that* true?

Every reality, every single dimension that is occurring right now is perfection in Divine motion. Every single one. **Every single outcome is positive and working toward growth.** Is that not a perfect mechanism?

The irony is, if you can let go of the "idea" of perfection—in essence, that you must *make* something (a situation or person) a certain way for you to be happy—you will accept perfection as the natural state of the Universe. And as you are a part of this vast Universe, you will know perfection in every cell of your body.

Once you realize perfection in the smallest quanta of your body—which is a microcosm of the entire Universe—your health will get better, you will rise often and well without the use of the word, and your rate of attraction and manifestation will improve exponentially.

Still do not meditate? Please stop reading right now, and take a few minutes to silence your mind and feel the perfection inside you. You may do this in a sitting or lying position, or you may walk or run or do yoga or sweep floors or golf—your bodily state does not matter in meditation; it is your mind that we want you to learn how to clear and to be in a receptive state of knowing and allowing.

Stop saying you need to find time to meditate, when you could clear your mind in the middle of a traffic jam if you chose to. Be present, and empty your thoughts every now and then, and soon, you will notice more and more moments of vacancy, which become longer and longer until you live in a state of emptiness in your mind (not your brain, as your brain will keep things functioning as the perfect mechanism that it is!).

This enlightenment is just that: emptying the mind until you *feel* lighter and lighter. You may lighten the body, as well, through less dense foods and consistent movement. Stop calling it "diet and exercise," please. It is all a part of enlightenment.

Lighten up, and know you are perfect, as is.

## LESSON #73: CARING FOR THE PLANET

How do you care for your planet?

Everyone does it in a different way, and many don't do it at all. You care for your body; why would you not care for the large body of dirt that you currently inhabit?

Some are actively "fighting" to preserve your so-called "environment." And yet, as we have taught you—and many teachers before us have taught—*what you fight continues.* What you resist, persists. Nothing happens through force. We mentioned that in our first book.

Yes, there are those who are polluting your planet with all kinds of chemicals and destructive elements. And yet, the earth is also very resilient, as is your body! As your cells are always multiplying and shedding, so is the smallest kernel of dirt on your earth. Trust that your planet knows how to heal itself. Even what you see as destructive storms—tornados, earthquakes, tsunamis, fires, and hurricanes—are all processes to purge and renew your earth's natural systems. If there were no people inhabiting the planet, these would not be seen as "bad" things. Only when such processes affect people are they deemed destructive.

Now, as you are evolving and your personal life is getting better and better—as those around you are feeling your Light and lifting their vibration in your presence or moving away from your frequency if it is too far in discrepancy—we ask you to include your planet in your visualizations and meditations.

Imagine Earth coated in bright, healing Light, regenerating its energy on its own. Trust that it knows how. Do this daily. Even if you take a moment in your day, perhaps when you are in your car at a stoplight, picture your planet bathed in the purest Light you can imagine, and feel your heart connected to all those who inhabit her.

We are calling the earth a female because she is receptive to this form of energy. I have been female more times than I've lived lives as a male, and so I can identify with the earth's energy. I have wandered the earth extensively in my many incarnations, and I feel I know her intimately, like a lover.

I was an avid gardener and grew my food throughout most of my lifetimes. We all would suggest you do the same. Get rid of your dependence on big superstores to offer you their chemical-laden food. Much of it we wouldn't even call "food." It is a promise of disease to eat much of what you ingest into your body. Don't put it into the earth, and you won't ingest it into your body. Use natural methods to repel bugs from eating your edible plants. Or get creative, and use other means. Chemical modifications are never the answer.

Love the earth as if she were your child or your mother. If you don't like children or your mother, love the earth because she gives you *life* here as you know it.

We find it amusing that your scientists keep looking for life on other planets with water. They are only looking for people who look *just like you do*. How arrogant! There are millions of life forms; they just don't look like you and don't require the same sorts of air, food, and water. They seem "invisible" to you only because you are far outside their frequency. As you learn to adjust this as a collective whole, you will find evidence of their appearance.

As you continue to rise and ascend into new levels of being and existence, perhaps one day, you will no longer require sustenance such as air, food, and water. Where we belong, without bodies, we require none of those things, and so we are not tied to a survival existence.

As you give to others for their basic survival needs, you will also move toward freedom, as you all will be in a closer vibrational gap to the "other side"—the way station where you go when you discard this body and "live" between lifetimes and heal and manifest at will.

Until then, work on lifting your vibration daily. Garden, eat your own plants, or support organic local farms. Wander well and often, whether in your neighborhood or around the globe. Please do not say you cannot afford to travel. *You were designed to travel.* You were never meant to stay in one place. If you feel that way in this lifetime, you are simply holding yourself back from growth, and perhaps you will learn this freedom of wandering in a new lifetime story.

Go back to basics, and manifest a means to wander, as Pilara often recommends. Make it a priority among gathering physical "things," which will also hold you back, and which you cannot take with you into the other realms.

Michelle has been focusing her meditations on images of white sandy beaches and teal waters, as we have mentioned. How many of you let yourselves do this? It is a very fun, imaginative exercise, and a relaxing meditation, as well, even if you never go there in reality. As she felt the warm waters and tasted the salty air and saw the colors of the sky and the ocean, she felt at peace and excited at the same time—a very nice sensation!

Because she was in this state, she drew toward her an email from a company that hires yoga instructors to teach in foreign lands on the beach in exchange for residence at an all-inclusive resort for the teacher and a guest. Airfare and a minor gift expense for the resort are the only requirements. Michelle found an extremely low rate for airfare that was only available on the day they purchased it!

Michelle had done this same sort of arrangement several years ago, and yet she somehow forgot the opportunity existed until she was in a state to receive it! She had not received emails from the company in years. And if she hadn't just visualized the perfect scenario, she might have put that email into the trash and not paid attention.

Now she and Jodah are going to a five-star resort in Cancun in October for a week! She will teach yoga once a day in a thatched bungalow over the ocean each morning, and she will have the rest of the day to play.

And so, if you are telling yourself you cannot wander, that you do not have the money, you are believing in lack, which is simply not true. Let go of *how* it will all happen for you, continue to visualize the dream, and believe it is happening, because it already *is* in another parallel dimension—you just have to reach it with your frequency.

## Lesson #74: Money is a By-product of Joy

Actually, everything that has manifested into form—that you deem a pleasurable source of energy, such as money—is a by-product of joy.

You believe you need money to have joy, but it is the other way around. Experience joy each day, and you will have an abundance of not just paper or metal currency—but *real* abundance and plenty …

Plenty of food, plenty of fun, plenty of friends, plenty of Love—plenty, plenty, plenty!

Once you *feel* plenty, you will naturally want to *give* plenty, and so it is self-sustaining joy.

How do you find joy? By declaring it, even in the midst of your so-called suffering, because all suffering is an illusion created in order to force you into a learning situation.

Remind yourself that while pain feels real, suffering is an illusion, and you may find joy in the midst of your suffering.

Suffering is more likely sourced from your man-made, created story around something that happened to you, rather than the true pain of what happened to you.

It happened, it's over, and you may find a lesson in it, and you may not learn the lesson until you leave this plane. It is of no matter.

Find the joy. Seek it out. Find it in both the small and big pleasures of the planet, in the quiet as well as the loud moments. Be with others who find joy in all, joy in the experience, joy in nature and pets and natural beauty; joy in the taste, touch, smell, and sounds of your natural world, as well as your animals, your people, your foods, your clothing, your _____. (Please fill in the blank.)

The more you list out things to be joyful about, the more your "filter" will focus on things to be joyful about. The more joy you have, the more money will show up for you. Just don't dwell on the money and make it an obsession, for then you will miss the joys all around you.

## Lesson #75: Resistance Training

Michelle and Jodah have been "working out" their bodies by lifting weights and moving and stretching their bodies at the gym they recently joined.

When your body lifts weights, it literally "breaks down" the tissues in order that they may be repaired and made even stronger.

*What if you did this to your emotional body?* In fact, you do it all the time in this entry-level dimension of yours. When you encounter something that feels "heavy" to you, as in contrasting your natural state of joy, you can practice resistance training through radical acceptance of all that is, knowing you will indeed become stronger through the challenge when you learn—once and for all—to fully let go.

All of Michelle's lessons most recently have been to let go and surrender. God is not "doing" this to her in order to teach her. She set this up for herself before she was born, in order to learn and grow and live her highest and best life. The Universe is simply matching the frequency of whichever "station" she is on. So when she is feeling "down" and is experiencing low self-worth tendencies, she is bringing to her "not-so-fun" stuff. And if she practices her "resistance training" by accepting the weight and LIFTING IT HIGHER, she draws to her all the "fun" stuff—like the brand new sports car she manifested! (More on that later.)

When the stories in your life leave you feeling defeated—don't give up, LIFT it up! Rise higher—acknowledge fully where you are, yes, but then use your tools to rise, rise, and rise some more, as we wrote extensively about in our first book.

There is no timeline in this, by the way. There is no time, remember? If you wallow around in other people's judgment and opinions—*or your own*—for a while, so be it. Sooner or later, you'll get sick of feeling so gross (original definition of "gross" is: *from Middle English*-"thick, massive, bulky")—and hopefully, you'll "pop" back up again, like a cork out of a bottle.

The grosser you feel, the more you will sink. The lighter and freer you feel, the higher you rise. If you are feeling heavy and gross, lift it up as you would a weight. See yourself as a weight lifter, a spiritual champion.

Please write down what feels like a weight to you in this moment, and what you might do to lift it up.

## Lesson #76: Individuation and Transmutation

Carl Jung, among other psychologists, considered "individuation" as a process of transformation, by bringing the personal and collective unconsciousness into consciousness. In this way, the person becomes whole and complete.

"Transmutation" is the process of transformation from one state into another form, one element into another, or one species into a new one. Alchemy, the early chemistry that most commonly turned base metals into form, is one such example of transmutation.

You are *all*—every single one of you—going through a transmutation on a grand scale.

Many of you are calling this an act of ascension—and it is, in a way. But moreover, you are not so much "moving up," as changing at your *cellular level of density*.

You may have heard about alkalizing the body through the foods you eat. And yet, we would like for you to understand that a pH—as in the measurement of acid levels in the body—stands for "potential hydrogen." So while a pH less than 7.0 is considered acidic and a pH of 7.0 is considered neutral, pH is defined as the measurement of electrical resistance between negative and positive ions in the body. (More on ions later in this book.)

This refers to your ionic *charge*, and how you manipulate your energetic core through the **mind** and your beliefs—in essence, "lightening" up the body so you eventually need no food at all and may move into—not higher, per se—but *faster moving dimensions*, you see.

Early alchemists created transmutation "circles" to protect from negativity during the process. Their "law of equivalent exchange" stated that matter could only be turned into matter, water into water, etc., or there would be grave consequences. Such circles and stories are now part of your modern mythological culture, through anime.

You can "alchemize a situation" by stepping inside it and transmuting it from the inside out. Ask your higher Self what is bugging you—discover the "gem" of understanding/learning that the situation has to offer—and then morph it into what you want to make manifest in your life.

You already know how to do this. We've given you many tools by now, the primary ones being meditation and visualization—and if you still aren't using those, we'd like to postulate why you might be struggling.

*You don't need any circles to keep negativity away from you.* Such symbols suggest you need to protect yourself from some greater fear, and so, in essence, you are creating *more* fear and attracting those very negative forces you are trying so hard to protect yourself from!

The reason you may be struggling with transmuting your fear into faith is that your complete cycle—the real "circle" here—of individuation requires you to be pushed from the "herd" mentality into self-actualization by following your "vocation," as Jung called it. We prefer calling it "passion through intuition."

When you are following your passion by listening to your intuition, you will **rise up** from the pack, and it will *feel* as if you are very much alone. And you will be, in Truth, for a while. Those in the pack will do everything to stay there, and as you rise, there will be a period when you will stray and be ostracized. And that is okay.

It will not *feel* okay. Not in the least! And yet, it is here where we would like to bring together the disparate parts of your psyche and *remember* **you are part of the whole**. In this way, you *become* the whole.

As you integrate with the ALL, you will lose the ego, and the ego will fight. You will process all manner of doubts and fears and negativity, and no amount of symbolic circles can protect you from this. Some will not make it all the way. And others—including *you* if you've read this far—will make it through to the other side of it, where a new level of authenticity, confidence, and *completion* arrives!

You will *feel* complete, because you are. And yet, from here, you will have so much more to do, but it will not *feel* like doing—more like BE-ing. All the time—just being.

So if you are in the midst of this alchemical transmutation of individuation (isn't *that* a mouthful of your descriptive words and labels), please KEEP GOING. Journal your dreams, as they will be powerful sources of integration for you right now.

Continue aligning with your "new" vision, *especially* when you feel that pit of despair in your stomach—the third chakra energy vortex of "power." Work your alchemical magic in yourself *first*, and it will help all others in the collective unconscious.

## Lesson #77: Symbolism in Everything

We know we just told you *not* to create symbols for everything, and yet, if you look at your world from our greater vantage point, you will see it speaks to you—as a hologram—as it **reflects** to you what you are thinking at any given time.

An example of this is Michelle's current decision/dilemma of changing up her hair color. It seems like a small change, but to a woman in your American society, it is an important identity distinction of creativity and beauty, yes? It was in our time, as well…

Michelle's hairdresser chose to make her hair go from a darker color on top gradually into her platinum blonde, but when it was done, Michelle did not like it at all! She decided to give her mind time to adjust to the dramatic change, but when she showered this morning and looked in the mirror, she did *not* like what she saw.

She is fixing the "error" tomorrow, and yet, when we told her to look for the symbolism, she laughed out loud. Michelle has been in and out of a "dark" state from her interactions with her teenage daughter, with whom currently she is not on the same vibrational wavelength. And so, as she is using tools to gradually return to the "Light"—of which she already *is*—her hair reflected where she is!

Another example is Michelle's new sports car that she recently manifested. She has never owned a sports vehicle, and when she was driving the car to the hair salon, she realized she felt a "oneness" with the car—she could feel all the bumps in the road, but it didn't matter. Unlike a sedan, which drives more smoothly, the sports car is designed to "hug" the road.

What does this mean, bigger picture?

For Michelle, she learned that when she feels a oneness with all that is, it may feel a bit "bumpier," but it is really embracing the "road."

What are some examples of symbolism in your life story at the moment?

## Lesson #78: Your Circle of Friends

Your closest circle of friends shows you where you are at any given time by reflecting your vibe back to you.

A small amount of you have life-long friends who have grown with you over time, and that is your expectation, as reflected in movies and television media. And yet, more often, if you are growing and changing, as you naturally do, your friends will change and reflect your newer frequencies.

Please don't let this alarm you! You are never, ever alone. You must know this by now. There are literally thousands of spirits circulating around you at any given moment, and you may tune into them as you wish. You also need remember that as you are all ONE, in the collective unconscious and through Spirit, you are all very connected, like the World Wide Web! Tap into *that* feeling of oneness, and it should alleviate any loneliness as you transition from one friend to another.

You will encounter many, many kindred souls on your journey here. Some you've known throughout lifetimes, some are meant to teach you brief but important lessons, and a select few may remain by your side as you travel through the ups and downs of your life, reminding you of the Love you share.

Always cherish the Love, for again, it is who you *are*, and so it feels very good. As you amplify the Love with others, you will find more to love together. That is the whole point of living.

## LESSON #79: DIVINE VESSELS

You are all Divine vessels for the most beautiful, creative inspiration possible—the only thing "in the way" is you and your belief in your sad stories. Allow for higher wisdom to flow through, and you will live out a higher way of being. Be and allow, be and allow, allow then be. That's a life well lived!

And the others? Allow *them* to just be.

Allow each other's stories to shape who they become. If you don't, they will remain like a lump of clay. Allow their suffering to show them the Truth of their being, the part of them you all share. Don't stay with them in their pain. Show them your highest Truth of your being, and live that out loud! Demonstrate, then see them in their highest Light, and soon they will match your vision. Or not. That is not up to you. Just keep seeing their inner Light grow and shine brighter.

If you are telling yourself a story about unforgiveness—about someone who you deem has harmed you, or it is you who may have harmed another—remember you came here with a story to live out, complete with "bad guys and good guys," with conflict and drama and heroes and heroines. You decided to learn lessons of compassion and strength and integrity and grace. You came here to remember. You came here to **rise up** out of all of it.

Everyone in your path is teaching you these things. You planned it, and you are learning it now. It won't be forever, as you have been taught—just for this lifetime—for you now know there is something more, something beyond the suffering cycle of learning and growth.

Pat yourself on the back now. Consider how you've survived all the dramas you created carefully for your soul's highest and best potential. You did it! You may have some more lessons along the way, but you will see them differently now you know that on the "other side"—in the way station and beyond, where we reside in the faster-moving dimensions that don't require a body—you will find utter bliss and joy *without even trying*.

You could get close to this now, just by remembering.

Focus on the appreciation, the gratitude, the peace that comes from these emotions. What is the result for you? Harmony? Joy? What is it for you? Please write this down, and next time your mind returns to your sad stories, please remember the real Truth. Return to appreciation, and you will find joy.

## LESSON #80: PEACEFUL AND POWERFUL

Your true strength lies in your ability to be both peaceful *and* powerful, at the same time.

Many of you would argue that it's just not possible. And that is the exact problem, you see. Your power lies in your ability to be at peace, to not have to be "right" all the time.

When you find you can go all day without telling a sad story about yourself or another, about the state of affairs in your community, your city, your world, then you are at peace. Your mind has the ability to stay open, and when you are in an open state, you are also in your power.

Power is not in the overcoming of something or someone. You will see that when you die. If you are all one, what is there to overcome? Power arises from affirming you are already strong, you are already brave, you already have integrity. If your mind is open, you are living a life of honesty. You don't need to attract any more lessons, but if you do, you know it is okay, for you've done it before—for eons—and can do it again.

Power is in rising above situations that, in the past, might have held you back. You empower yourself by remembering this, and then putting it into practice again and again, over and over, until you live in a state of empowerment. When you do, you will radiate and embody empowerment, and there will be those in awe of this state who will copy it, and those who will be blinded by it.

Be empowered anyway. The blind are that way of their own accord. Don't seek to "convert" them—or anyone else, for that matter—to your ways. You empower others by living in a constant state of empowerment.

Right now, you are most likely in a state of "betterment," as you are reading this book and seeking to make yourself a "better" person. That is good, for at its core, you are really seeking a higher vibratory state that *feels* better.

Reach for the better feeling state until you feel absolutely amazing and incredible! Then amplify it, and amplify it some more until you can't take it; you're extremely happy! That happy state is also your power. Own it. Bathe in it. Be one with it.

You are doing more for humanity by empowering yourself than you ever will by battling yourself or another. You are all connected, you are all one, and if you are at peace—you will ALL be at peace.

# The Book of Myagana

## Lesson #81: Lasers of Light

Laser is an acronym for "light amplification by stimulated emission of radiation." It's a device that emits light through a process of optical amplification based on the stimulated emission of electromagnetic radiation. It differs from other sources of light in that it emits light coherently.

Okay, enough with the scientific explanation. What we would like to offer is that lasers are focused light. You use them for a variety of purposes, such as in medical procedures and computer printers, but we would like for you to understand the application of them from our perspective.

You are all beings of Light. You are more light than you are matter, and yet, you will not realize the enormity of this fact until you leave your body.

We, as The Power of 10, are complete beings of Light. We established that early on, as we have surpassed this human experience to come together as the same wavelengths, to teach and expand your reality rapidly, before you destroy it.

You can focus your Light as we do. We must focus our amplified Light in order to reach Michelle, and she must lift her vibration to meet us. We are currently focusing our laser-focused beams of Light, Love, and higher energy frequencies to lift and engage her. She is mired in the drama of her story she created before birth, and her ego is recognizing it as real.

We cannot speak through her when she is in this state. She believes the lies told by others that she is not good enough. They are all just projections of fragile, infantile egos. And yet, in her weakened state, she has become deluded and ill.

We are focusing our Light toward her now. We have the precision of a laser, which is science you may comprehend from this point in your evolution. When you know of others who have been weighed down by the perceived trauma of a situation—which is really just a storyline—you may also gather together with like-minded, like-vibrating others to focus your Light together and lift them.

You are not enabling in this way. You are not interfering with the life lessons they chose in their soul's agreement pre-birth(s). No, you are sharing your collective Light. It is the best way to raise humanity at this juncture, one soul at a time.

Many of you would liken this to prayer. If the intention is pure, prayer can be of a positive nature. But do not say you are going to pray for someone and then don't actively do it. If you want to pray, do not "beg" a personified version of your God to do something for you or them. When you pray, envision them enveloped in Light and encased in Love. Take a few minutes to really imagine them in this way, for this is the Truth of who they really are. This is the Truth of who *you* really are. You share this Truth. You are both beings of Light, currently experiencing life lessons in a body of matter. You are pure energy, and energy never dies, it just changes form.

Matter recycles—your body may be recycled into the earth, but your soul lives on as part of Spirit, which is a positive force that grows the Universe.

Many would call me, Myagana, a leader. And yet, that choice of words does not really fit me correctly. The energies of the 10 all match perfectly, and I was the first to step forward with the intention to teach all of you. That is how we all came together—through a shared mission and intention, and through sharing the same exact frequency. We are all on the same channel, so to speak.

We would like for you to practice sending lasers of Light energy to someone who is "down," who is allowing perceived external circumstances to weigh down their energetic vibration. You have the power to do this, which should not affect your energetic emissions whatsoever. You are not *giving* them your energy, per se. You are lending your shared Light, which brightens both of you.

## LESSON #82: YOUR BODY IS LIKE A PRISM

Because your body takes in—reflects and refracts—light, in essence, it is more like a prism than a mound of dirt.

Why do you think your chakras, the energy centers in the body and aura known by ancients and seers, are the colors of the rainbow?

Refraction is, in essence, when a faster medium runs into a slower medium, the velocity may be changed, but not the frequency.

So when you are feeling and living the higher vibrations, and you encounter something or someone of a much lower vibration, you may think they are "bringing you down," but in Truth, you are allowing them to "slow" you down, but no one or no *thing* can change your frequency.

The exception to this is your thoughts surrounding a person or situation. If you allow your "story" to rule your mind, you will create your very own lower vibrational frequency and attract all manner of unpleasant situations and people into your inner circle.

How do you climb out? Remember the rules of refraction—your frequency can't be changed except by you. Change your thoughts around the person or situation. Tell a new story, one that includes the things and experiences and people you are grateful for. Talk about the wonderful lessons you've gained from this experience/person/situation. Talk more about how you see things now in a new perspective, and that your vibration will only go higher and higher when you let go of the things you can't control—WHICH IS EVERYTHING—except your own thoughts.

Do the things that make you happy, even when you are feeling not so happy. Michelle was feeling sad over the death of a former boyfriend, and she was telling herself a story of how he was too young and that he lived a reckless life. And yet, when she did some morning yoga and silenced her mind in meditation, he came to her and said quite clearly, "Be happy for me. No one is ever gone forever."

Those who have gone on before you are pure Love and Light. Do not be sorry for the termination of this particular life story—they are not sorry. They are living in the purity of their Light, in the full expression of their "prism," reflecting many colors of Light and energy back to you if you are in a position to receive it.

Make a list now of any loved ones who have passed before you. What do they represent? What lessons did their presence in your life story teach you? Can you feel them now? What if you silence your mind, can you feel them now? Can you sync up to their higher vibratory state?

Even those spirits who haven't fully transitioned and are focused on earthly attachments are still lighter vibrationally than you are, simply because they have discarded the heaviness of the body. You may still live in close harmony with their soul, and they are in an even better position to teach you from where they are, which is nothing like how they were while in the body. All ego leaves with the body. All that remains are certain individual character traits that will let you know who they were in body—they are more Spirit than body. They are more Light than matter. So are you. Learn from those in Spirit.

## Lesson #83: Singularity

Everything you are is everything you need.

You may want to write this down: Everything I am is everything I need.

The more you live this Truth, the more—ironically—every single thing you could ever want or desire is drawn toward you, as if you were in the center of a black hole.

In the middle of a black hole in space, your physicists would say that all of your "laws" break down. The gravitational field is so intense that no matter or radiation can escape. It is like a giant vortex in space, or a "whirlpool" in one of your oceans. You can't fight it. It is named "singularity."

The same is true if you see yourself as one with the field of pure consciousness. You see, when you are beyond using our tools, and the tools of other teachers, and you live in a pure state of knowing you are all that you need, you will *draw* all you need.

It's that simple.

As you are spiritually evolving past the limits of the body, you are realizing you started your ascension through language. You rose up as you understood that your thoughts created your reality. You began to question your society's belief systems and realized you were limitless. You "got" that you are connected to everyone else. And then, you became one with all that is.

Once you reach what many consider the "God" state, in which all of your senses are heightened, you feel transcendent, in that no person or situation bothers you or can bring down your frequency; you continue rising higher and higher. You are God, you are Love, you are Source energy—whatever you call it, it doesn't matter anymore—because your language only served to move you past "cavemen" times.

You see, again, all dimensions are occurring at the very same time. Lift your vibration higher each day, and connect with the highest version of You in each moment, and you will draw all manner of fun toward yourself like a singularity. All earthly laws shall break down by this time, and no one will know what to do with you, and that is okay. You will be a Light for which they may aspire. And if not, you can just be a Light.

## Lesson #84: Pulling into Differing Energy Fields

As we stated in the first book, your people appear to be polarizing in opposite directions. We have compared it to the yolk of an egg, sinking due to its density, while the whites of an egg are much lighter and frothier.

And yet, now that you have a deeper understanding of how things really are, we'd like to point out to you that it is not permanent, this separation. How can it be, when you are all connected, and all are one?

Your energies are simply being pulled into different dimensional frequencies. If you remember that underneath it all, at the core of your being, you are Light—then you may conceive of yourselves as fluid as light waves.

As you think a thought, and it becomes a belief and then an opinion by your focus on it, then perhaps an action, it may be in direct opposition to someone else's thought-belief-opinion-action.

That is why you can live in the same exact world and experience very different versions of reality.

One is not right or wrong, it all just *is*.

What is necessary, then, is a total integration. See if you might integrate *all* of the parts of yourself, and love them, every piece of you—even the darkest parts. In fact, especially the darkest parts! Those dark parts of you need Light the most, and if you can shine it onto yourself, you shine for all humankind.

Jodah asked Michelle last night as they were about to fall asleep, if she thought humanity was sinking so we all can "boomerang" back up again—as we have suggested in other sessions in regard to your personal process and life journeys.

And we would like to pose it this way—you are all a microcosm of the macrocosm of the Universe. As you personally learn to reach your lows, then bounce back into your highs, you will eventually learn to even out your energies and find balance and equilibrium in all things. As you are all experiencing this as a whole, of course you will find it on a bigger level—in your communities, towns, cities, countries, etc. Remember, please, that all those "designations" of city and country are *man-made*! In Truth, there are no boundaries now, are there? You are **one**.

And so, as you learn to integrate, all of collective unconsciousness shall integrate. When the world can shine Light on its darkness, the world will find its equilibrium and know peace. And peace is what we're all about.

## Lesson #85: Global Upgrade

You upgrade your cell phones more often than you upgrade your beliefs.

Let's explore that.

Why would you think your technology needs to change faster than your thinking? Technology cannot think for you. You must program your computers, right? Someone does. And so we'd like to recommend to you that from time to time you take a good look at your belief systems and see if they couldn't use an upgrade.

When you think a thought, ask yourself where it came from. Was it from a book, a television show, a friend, work? Was it a judgment? Did it come from a teaching you learned in childhood, or was it more recent? How often have you had this same thought? Has it made its way into your "hard drive" as a belief? If you could pose it as a belief, how would you write it down?

Please jot down your firmest beliefs in your journal. Please do this; don't put it off—even if all you can think of is the one belief that comes to mind in the moment.

Here's an example that came to Michelle's mind:

"People are inherently good."

That has been a thought occurring over and over again in her mind because she was recently at the receiving end of a lot of blame and judgment, and so she actively turned her mind toward this statement, and so here it is.

Although, we might counter, that "good" is a judgment. There is, in Truth, no good or bad, no right or wrong. There are only "lessons" from where you stand, not doled out by an angry deity or by karma, but more as an energetic balancing act. Once you learn to integrate *all* the parts of you without judgment, you will find your "heaven on earth" that many have prophesied. Turn a flashlight on those wounded areas of yours, and know that at the root of you, you are part of a positive, growth-oriented Universe that is ever expanding.

And so, an upgraded thought to Michelle's belief might be:

"People are inherently positive."

This is more like Truth, wouldn't you say? Because if the Universe is ever-expanding, it is moving in a positive direction. If you are negative, you are going against the natural, organic flow of all that is—and so, it doesn't feel very good at all. If you are a microcosmic part of the macrocosm of the Universe, you, too, are positive. Being positive is what you are made up of.

See if you might upgrade more of your thoughts, beliefs, and opinions in your journal. If you are in a group setting, please allow the moderator to begin this talk.

## LESSON #86: SELFISHNESS

It is your selfishness, your greed, which impedes your progress toward peace. It is an insistence that ego is everything, when ego is a delusion—a distorted sliver of Spirit. All you have to do is open to the greater portion of You—the highest You who came here to learn and be. Stop getting in the way of your growth by acting like a toddler and demanding everything goes your way.

Manifest through surrender, then give it all away as if it were unlimited, because in Truth, it *is* unlimited.

Define your definition of "Self" to be inclusive of all others, and then you will feel complete and whole. Selfish is not the same as self-full. Know the difference.

Please take a few moments to write down the difference between being and acting selfish vs. self-full. What do those two terms mean to you? How can you be more self-full today and serve yourself as a part of the whole?

## Lesson #87: Running Compassion

Most lessons are about "running" compassion, not anger or fear.

What do we mean by "running"? Not as in running away from something, more like running a faucet of water or running an ongoing audio recording.

All your lessons come back to this: compassion. Often your dictionaries define it as something akin to empathy or sympathy. And yet, the original meaning comes from Latin: *to love together with.*

Empathy allows you to feel what another is feeling. Sympathy has you feeling bad for another's circumstances. Compassion asks you to know that the other is also in you, and therefore, you love them as you love yourself, *through* everything, for you *are* everything.

Compassion has the word "passion" in it, and so, if you do this with passion, you are igniting a flame and acting from a place of inspiration, not because you feel "sorry" for someone else's plight, but because you, too, have suffered similarly throughout many lifetimes, and you wish to move beyond into an over-reaching Love that is unconditional and a unifying force.

And so, practice today running a "tape" of compassion and see where it takes you. It is a radical form of acceptance—not tolerance, as that would suggest that you're simply "putting up" with something or someone. Rather, radical acceptance allows for embracing it *all* for exactly what it is.

Who and what can you love together with today?

## Lesson #88: Manifest Greatness (Not Stuff)

Once you have mastered manifesting all manner of play things—from cars to houses to vacations to clothing and whatever it is your heart desires—eventually, you might reach a place of complacency where such things don't account for much. They are not "bad," per se, as they gave you momentary pleasure—which is never a bad thing, right?

And yet, you came here for so much more than that! You came here to manifest GREATNESS.

What is "greatness" to you? Please define it in your journal.

What is your caliber?

What is your character like? If you could describe yourself—your ego personality—as the main character in a story, what traits would you list? Write them down.

At the end of your life, what could you say about yourself that defined your greatness? Was it the amount of stuff you garnered? Was it how much you gave away? Was it the pleasure you found in each moment? Was it the fame or friends you found along the way? What would you like your greatness to look like?

## Lesson #89: Try NOT to Smile

I would like to show you an experiment today. When you really want to do something, try doing its opposite first.

For an example, if you are unhappy at this moment, try *not* to smile.

Do you see how this works? Did you smile?

You see, the Universe "hears" you (if the Universe was a person and had ears, which it does not) in only positive terms. And so, if you try not to do something, all the Universe "hears" (as in matching the frequency of) is SMILE.

When you are making an effort *not* to eat, as in a strict form of dieting, all the Universe hears and lines up with is EAT. If you are trying NOT to spend or do drugs or call your ex-lover, all the Universe aligns with is the exact thing you are avoiding.

And so, choose a different vibe with this. If you would like to lose weight, perhaps say, "I now see myself healthy, thin, fit, and full of vitality!" How does that make you feel versus "I need to lose weight"?

If you'd like to manifest more abundance, do not focus on your debt. That is dwelling on the lack of it, which will only amplify MORE lack of it … are you understanding? This is important. Instead of saying you need more money or that you need to pay off your bills, perhaps affirm to yourself daily: "I have all that I need." "My life is filled with examples of abundance." "I live a most fruitful life, and I appreciate all that I have."

Please take a few moments to list those things and experiences you'd like to have at this moment, and word them in a positive way, so that the Universe may line up with your new vibrational offering.

## Lesson #90: Playing With Your Energy Field

As we have pointed out so often, you are more than just your body.

Your inner energy emanates out for several feet (in your frame of measurement). Some call this your "aura." Whether or not you are sensitive enough to see it or see any colors within it doesn't matter. You can still play with it to your betterment.

Michelle was in Zumba class yesterday, and she was in a bad mood. Someone had disappointed her, and she was creating a sad story around it rather than seeing it as the simple frequency change it was. She's still learning. So she went to Zumba class to make herself feel better and shift her energetic vibrational offering.

It worked for a little while, until Michelle began to feel as if the person next to her and the person in front of her were closing in on her. She felt as if she was suffocating, and she felt angry that they were not aware enough to move away. In reality, they were probably just in their own little world, or subconsciously attracted to her inner Light, as we were enjoying Zumba with her! But rather than stewing in these emotions, or speaking up and setting a boundary (the music was too loud), she pretended she was in a giant bubble of energy and "blew it up" until it expanded out in all directions from her dancing body.

It worked! The woman to the left of her moved over significantly more to the left, where there was ample space. And the woman in front of her left the class mid-way!

This is not to say you should manipulate your energy to make people leave, but if you need some space, this is a useful tool, especially if you are sensitive to other people's energies as your base vibrational offering is lifted.

You may also do this so as not to be noticed. Try imagining you are invisible in a crowd and watch how powerful your mind is! Pretend you have a cloak around you that covers not just your body, but 2-3 feet in every direction.

Sometimes, you all just need a little space to gain clarity and focus. When you leave this body behind, and you move toward the way station and beyond, this will not matter, as your energetic frequencies merge with all that is. You harmonize with like-vibing others, as we have done.

But for now, please play with these tools we are offering and have fun with them! Don't be too concerned if it doesn't work at first. Keep trying, and don't put too much effort into it, or you will take all the fun out of it.

# THE BOOK OF PILARA

## LESSON #91: WANDERING IS GOOD FOR YOUR SOUL

When you are wandering, whether it is through travel or through simply walking around with no agenda, you are in closest harmony with your soul.

Your soul wants nothing more than to be free. You assign the meaning of freedom to money, but it is not little pieces of paper and metal that will give you freedom. Not having to be anywhere and taking in the beauty of your natural world will give you the most freedom. When you are in a state of freedom, you are in the same vibrational countenance as your soul, which is part of the great Spirit where you come from.

There are some who stubbornly refuse to move anywhere, who say they are "happy" with where they are, and that they don't "like" to travel. And we would say, you cannot NOT move! Your body, your cells, and the very atoms that vibrate and oscillate within your cells, are always in motion. The earth you live on is always in motion; you just don't feel it now, do you? It's much bigger than you are. Your atoms are much smaller than the totality of you. Neither matters, each is in motion.

When you stay "stuck" by your stubborn refusal to make change or to move your body in exercise or dance or travel to new places, you resist the natural order of the Universe, which is always and forever expansion.

Why not try going with the flow? Go forward, whatever that means for you. Take a walk around the block, as we have suggested to you in the last book. Have you still been walking, or did you do it that one time when we suggested it?

Part of your freedom and the state of ease you so desire is the organic movement forward of your body. You will feel lighter. You will feel like more of the creator you were designed to be.

Again, if you say you "can't" because of (insert various excuses here), time constraints (there is no such thing as time—it is a man-made concept), money (another man-made concept and can be manifested by your belief in abundance and gratitude for all you have), a job you hate (find a new one that lights you up), a partner who no longer matches your frequency (attract one whose vibrational alignments supports and uplifts you both), your health (created by vibrational alignment rather than resistance) ...

Please list any excuses you have, followed by their opposite Truth.

## Lesson #92: It's Always About a Better Fit

It's always—ever and only—about being a better fit.

As you go through your life and experience it in moments, there will be those who do a better job of "sticking" within an octave of your current vibrational frequency. Those who do have often shared many lives with you, and so they *feel* where you are at any given time and can match it easily.

Many, many more others will not, and that is all right, as long as you don't hold them to where you are.

The Buddhists and yogis would call this forming an "attachment," and we would agree here. Your attachments keep you from moving higher on the vibrational scale.

Just don't hold too tightly. If something or someone feels off, it usually is. You were designed with a built-in guidance system to see how harmoniously you match up with others. When it feels wrong, that means your inner alarms are going off, and you would do well to create some distance between you.

If that distance is already occurring—LET IT. Often this happens organically when people are not a match for each other, whether in a romantic relationship, professional relationship, or friendship. It doesn't matter what you label it—you were drawn together magnetically due to your vibrational offering, and if you're no longer feeling it, please let it go.

This does not mean "they" will be gone forever. It means that temporarily you are not a match. As they grow and so do you, you may come back together again, as so often happens. Please list a time when you were separated from another person who meant something to you, and you returned to each other. What was that like? Was there more to learn? Did you stay "together," or did you separate again? How did it feel when you first met, and how does it feel now?

Please spend some time writing about this. If you haven't found yourself in this situation, ask yourself who you would like to connect with now. Why do you feel this way? Is it "unfinished business"? Know that there is no such thing. You will eventually see them on the other side. And yet, if there is some lesson that you wish to tackle again, that is indeed why you came forward to this form of reality, so do it. Reach out and connect, and pay attention to the current vibes you are feeling—not just those you felt in your past.

## LESSON #93: PLANS VS. PEACE

It's always—ever and only—about finding your peace.

How do you find yours? Is it through resolution of a conflict? If the only time you find peace is when you resolve a conflict, you will continually feel an excess of suffering. All conflict is an illusion, arising from a need to be right.

What if you could find peace in this moment without your mind finding a conflict to reach peace *from*?

Allow peace to arise on its own, without having to overcome a challenge, and you will have a better chance of staying there once a challenge surfaces on its own.

Don't create a challenge for your mind to leap over. There are enough physical dangers in your world to keep yourselves busy in your lifetimes.

Do you find peace in the beauty of nature? If so, how often do you find yourself there?

This is not a judgment or a commentary on your choices. We would just like to point out that if your way to peace is through nature, then perhaps you should spend more time there.

Is there peace in your travels, or do you find conflicts even there? How do you react, for example, if your flight is delayed or your luggage is lost? Do you lose your peace?

When you have expectations of how things should be, you're not wandering, you are planning. Planning involves being in your head. Over planning kills the magic. Why not just follow where your heart takes you?

Trust you'll go the direction that teaches you the most or helps you find the most joy! Sure, go ahead and make reservations, but if something goes differently than your plans, have faith that you can still have fun.

The word "reservation" can mean *a booking arrangement* or *withholding your fears.* Make arrangements if you must, but let go of any fears that are keeping you back.

## Lesson #94: Differing Frequencies

When you talk to someone on a different frequency, it is the same as if you were speaking other languages or if they were hard of hearing; stop trying and wasting your energy. Either allow them to follow your lead or drift gently away. Nothing is worth giving away your peace.

Peace itself is contagious under the right conditions. If you are close enough in frequency, they will get what it is you are offering. If you are currently too far apart, it will literally hurt you if you try.

Stop trying so hard. Surrender and you will raise your levels of peace to be felt and amplified by those closest in range.

True mastery is "bringing it home" by being in the middle of all manner of vibrational offerings and not being affected whatsoever. It's not that you are above or below—you deflect and inherit, immerse and reject, until you know no such thing as polarity. This is a sign of the highest mastery, and you may need to die before you can achieve it.

If you can be blissed out no matter what is happening to you or around you, you've reached the "highest" level you can while still in the framework of a body. That is true success.

## Lesson #95: Freedom is Being Fully You

Freedom is knowing who you are at any given moment.

When things go "wrong," you have a saying—you're "only human." We would like to point out that saying is false.

You are only Spirit.

Now sometimes you *act* like the human character you chose, but if you keep affirming that you're "only human," you are offending your true Self, which is 100% Spirit.

You are more than your human personality—way more. When you think of yourself, please consider the vast Spirit that makes up all of eternity and infinity in your facsimiles of time and space.

Honor your soul, for sure—for it is the tiny spark of the Spirit, a wave in the giant ocean of life. And yet, your soul is one with Spirit, the same as you are One with each other.

And so, we return to the beginning of the lesson: you are only free when you know who you really are. Be fully *you*, and be free.

The real "you" doesn't have personality traits—those belong to the ego. And while they are not "bad" or "good," they are not the Truth of who you are, which is Spirit.

Therefore, what does being *you* mean to *you*? Please contemplate this question in today's meditation or write down the answer(s).

## Lesson #96: Perspective From a Plane

When you go on a trip, and you travel by airplane, do you ever notice how different things look from your higher vantage point as you are taking off or landing?

That is how your lives look to us, from a "higher" perspective. What if you viewed your life story in this way? How would it differ in emotion by looking at it from a higher place? Would your "problems" and challenges seem smaller?

You see, when you lift your vibration, you are entering new territory—a "place" where your challenges and lessons appear small in comparison to where you are going.

How does this life story look compared to alternate life stories you may construct? What if you tapped into those alternative options now? How might another life look to you, one with smaller issues and bigger payoffs?

Please describe that life story right now. If it already resembles what you are currently living out, that's okay, too. But please expand your vision of what is possible.

## Lesson #97: Ancient Cities

Have you ever been to a "historical" site with ancient ruins? How did it make you feel to be there, in the midst of a supposedly "ruined" civilization?

Knowing what you do now, that there is no such thing as "time" and that all things are happening simultaneously, those "ancient" cities and civilizations are *still happening as we speak!*

Cultures and societies around your world are *always* changing, always growing, always evolving as part of the ever-increasing movement of our Universe. Nothing is ever "ruined." When you feel sadness at the alleged passing of a civilization's moment in time, please remember that it is through the building and falling that your lessons have been learned. Perhaps what you are feeling is the true *greatness* of that culture—that is still happening NOW. Perhaps you shared another lifetime in that place, or in a similar "past" society, that has you feeling nostalgic.

Instead of the nostalgia, which is a longing for something that no longer exists, why not tap into the creative genius of that moment in created time and space, and let it fill you up and expand your spiritual growth?

Michelle felt something similar as she visited the ancient Mayan ruins in Tulum, Mexico. The little hairs on her arms all stood at attention, despite the humidity in the air, and she felt as if she wanted to cry with familiarity. Sometimes you humans weep when you are overwhelmed with emotion—whether "good" or "bad"—it doesn't matter. Such is the case with Michelle and her strong intuitive senses. She asked subconsciously what this all meant, this connection to a place she'd never seen before, where she seemed to know exactly where to go, despite never having visited. And she heard an answer, a voice that distinctly said, "You were a king."

Michelle then hoped she was a benevolent king, not one responsible for the fall of a great and wise civilization, at which we laughed heartily.

Nothing ever dies. Nothing ever goes away. It is all happening right now, in this very moment, simultaneously. Feel it, allow it to expand your soul. If you were once a king, it was your soul who chose that role to play in that particular lifetime to expand your soul, and therefore, expand outward the growth of the entire Universe. And so, if a city had to "fall," it was only to make room for the new, just the way it happens in your present lifetimes.

## Lesson #98: Why Travel and Wandering are Important

When you wander—truly wander—you get outside yourself.

Your journeying experiences are what you will "take with" you when you move into the beyond. Not the stuff you bought along the way, but the positive feelings you emanated as you moved out of your head and explored new places and territories.

Strangers along the way become friends who share their stories and move on. Even the sunsets look different from a new vantage point, yes? Same sky, different viewing platform.

Of course, you may over plan everything and miss out on the wonders of the flow of wandering ...

But I need to make reservations, right? I need to know where we're going, right? What if we get lost?

We can hear your thoughts as you think them, and they are getting in the way of your understanding.

The whole point is to get lost! Get a little lost and just see what happens. That's when the fun starts!

When Michelle and Jodah went on their first weekend getaway together to Mendocino, she convinced him to just drive and find a place to stay wherever they went. It was November and rainy, and so not so much of a "risk." (Although, they were prepared to sleep in the car if necessary.)

Instead, they found a small boutique hotel inside a huge Victorian, and because it was last minute, the owner gave them the top floor suite—with a jetted Jacuzzi tub overlooking the ocean, fireplace, and steam shower—at a bargain price!

It is the same place they went to this past weekend for their fourth wedding anniversary, but this time, they made reservations, and this time, the top suite was booked. So they stayed in a small room downstairs on one weekday and moved on to the neighboring city of Fort Bragg on the weekend.

When they paid the manager, he mentioned the suite that had been reserved was now open! The people cancelled last minute. But since Michelle and Jodah had already paid for the Fort Bragg room, they still had to go.

Of course, they had a wonderful time in Fort Bragg, as the people there gave them a suite overlooking the beach—complete with champagne and fresh flowers—for their anniversary! As they were happy and loving and of the highest frequency, they had fun wherever they went, even when they planned it.

When they got out of their heads and into their hearts, the best memories were made.

## Lesson #99: Being Stuck

There's a part of you that likes being unhappy if you tell yourself that you're happy being stuck. Wherever you don't feel freedom is where you start making changes—whether it's your job, the amount of money you make, your marriage, your friendships, whatever. If you're not moving—and growing and learning and creating—you're already dead.

Move your body in exercise, move your home, move your career forward, move your relationships deeper, travel and wander often—always move something or someone or somewhere ... be like the cells of your body, always dancing and renewing life!

Please jot down a list of things or people or situations you might move today. Perhaps start small, and work your way up toward things you *think* might take more effort. They don't. You just *think* they do. Write them down anyway, and check in with your feelings. Wipe away any fear or doubt or trepidation. Literally imagine using a rag or sponge and clearing those negative feelings away! Start getting excited NOW about how you might move things around or forward or through. Just move.

## Lesson #100: You Don't Need to Wander

We understand that we just spent several lessons instructing you to wander widely. And yet, now we will seemingly contradict ourselves by stating that, in Truth, you do not *need* to wander to leave your worries behind—do it now!

We would like you to wander because it is fun and enriching, because it serves you well to see how others with differing customs still share the same heart and Spirit. Your customs are manmade, but your souls are just variant expressions of one great source of Light and Love—*everywhere you go.*

So please do not wander to leave your troubles behind. That is a false premise, for your so-called "troubles" are a creation of the mind and will follow you wherever you travel. Wandering aimlessly is the opposite of that! Do so without *aim*. No targets, no destination—just be present, and watch the world and its inhabitants with awe and respect.

Your troubles are illusions. *Reality is what you make of it.* Make a new reality today, one where there are no "problems." Please make a short list of any "problems" you are currently facing, and ask how you might feel if they disappeared right now.

Now here's your exercise for today: feel the feelings of your problems being gone. Do whatever you can to be in that feeling state of having zero problems. If there is a challenge you are currently *choosing* to take on, that is of a different energetic frequency. Problems are more a perception of something that is happening *to* you, not something you are choosing to create.

Or are you?

Ask yourself if you are the one who is creating your problems, and then take steps today to alleviate them, for the same energy that created can also destroy.

If you are taking on a new challenge for the fun and discovery of it, then do so with a sense of play and not stress or fear or pressure. If it turns into those feelings, ask yourself why you are doing it.

# THE BOOK OF THERAS

## LESSON #101: WANTING WHAT'S BEST

When people speak of the Universe as a person wanting what's best for another, they are speaking of their perception of Love.

As has been reiterated again and again, since the Universe is in a continual state of expansion, of course you being at your highest vibrational state in any given moment is what creates the best and highest alignment with all. It is not a "wanting," you see, for the Universe is not a person and has no emotion or desire. It is a giant "state of being"—a force for continual growth.

When you feel Love for another, when you are wanting what's "best" for them, if it's unconditional, you won't envision what *you* might want for them, but what would best move them forward in growth and expansion, thereby harmonizing with the natural flow of all that is ...

When you feel romantic love, the same might be apparent. Yet often, the opposite is true, and what you deem romantic love is simply your attachment to another for the sake of your happiness and fulfillment.

*You cannot be filled by what you already are.* We've established that, haven't we? You are Love, therefore, you do not need to seek Love. You simply show your Love, and Love will attract Love.

If you are desperate for Love, you are demonstrating a lack of the one thing you really want, which is insane—because you are already it.

If you feel desperation around another, they are not meant for you, as they are on a differing "track" to their own destination. It does not mean forever, as they very well could cross paths with you again as they change and grow. And yet, it will not feel so good to be around them as they resist their own change and evolution.

If you can keep your Light shining through focusing on things and people and experiences that make you feel good, you can be in their midst during a transformation and lend a spark to their soul's expansion. And yet, if they don't want to expand, and you keep on expanding, eventually one or both of you will fall.

When Michelle was a little girl, she was learning to water ski for the first time with some friends. The well-intentioned father of her friend instructed her to "hold on no matter what" to the rope. This teaching helped her stand up on the skis, and yet, as she fell into the water, she still held on for as long as she could.

All that resistance—with the boat towing her at full speed and the water pushing against her face—almost drowned her. She lost her bikini bottoms and had to let go, which embarrassed her.

This is a funny story, but a good example of how when we hold on too fiercely to an attachment, eventually the opposing force of it will make you let go—or you will drown.

If Michelle had held on just long enough to stand up and enjoy the ride, and had let go only when she was tired of the experience, she might have had a better time of it.

Use your willpower and determination to lift you up and power up your existence, and when the time comes, let go and allow yourself to surrender the outcome. You know this, but it is time to live it in each moment.

Many of you are experiencing more and more "transcendent" moments of peace and Love—and we would say, "MORE OF THAT!" Allow the moment to remain as long as possible by being *fully aware* and present to the experience. The experience is one of **pure consciousness**! How might you describe it? How is it like Love? If you've had such an experience, please write down the details now. If not, perhaps spend some time in meditation and contemplation until you feel uplifted.

## LESSON #102: LUMINOUS FLUX

When you are one, you have limited Light output, yes? And when you connect with another with similar wavelengths, you double your outflow, yes?

Luminous flux is the quantity of the energy of light (emitted per second) in all directions. One unit of luminous flux is called a "lumen" (lm).

When you are solo, you are a lumen (which sounds an awful lot like "human," don't you think?). You are one being of Light in a field of many. When you join with another, and 10 more, and 10 more, you create a luminous flux that is powerful and unyielding.

How you feel your "lumen-ness" is by getting in touch with your inner Light, your Love for Self, for others. How you expand into a luminous flux is through resonating with others of similar light wavelengths (groups of protons, whatever you wish to call it) such as we do.

As The Power of 10, we do not "gather" each other into a group, per se. We emanate Light, and we come together organically. You may do this, too, although not to as great of an extent while you still exist within a body of matter. As you focus more on your Light body than your body of matter, you will see others in a new "light," and together, with a great deal of amplification, you cannot see darkness.

We will say that again.

You cannot see darkness.

If darkness is the absence of light, and you are amplifying your lumens, you cannot see its opposite.

We would call it a "law," but we have grown tired of your use of the word. It does not connote the higher Truth to which we are pointing.

Sometimes, your words cannot convey the meaning from which we hope to impart this wisdom.

"See" it for yourself. Practice today imagining yourself as a light bulb, and visualize turning your light higher and dimming it down, and see how it affects those around you. Journal your results, and then continue turning your imaginary light bulb up higher a little each day, until it feels "normal" for you to shine brightly.

There are only so many levels of this sort of Light amplification you may practice while still in a body. Gathering with others to amplify your Light together is recommended, so the rest of your world may know more Light than darkness.

## LESSON #103: TRUTH EQUATES FREEDOM

I see myself as a holy (or whole-y) vessel of/for Truth.

The word holy may be interchangeable with "sacred" if it carries too many religious connotations. Know that sacred has the same letters as "scared." It is the opposite of fear, no matter what your religious documents state to the contrary.

Repeat after me, please: I see myself as a sacred vessel of Truth.

I see myself as a sacred vessel for Truth.

Truth is all I am.

I am Truth, and so is everyone else.

The highest Truth carries no opposite and has no alternate perspective.

The Truth is never harsh. Jesus said, "The Truth shall set you free."

Truth equates freedom.

The Truth is that you are all that is. All that is is inside of you now. The only Truth is Now.

Truth and Spirit are interchangeable.

Truth and Spirit are composed of Love.

As you are Truth, and you are part of Spirit, you, too, are composed of Love.

If you are composed of Love, hate and intolerance will make you sick.

If you want radiant health and peace, affirm that you are Love, and Love is the Truth of all that is and all you are.

## Lesson #104: Zefluetic Balance

We know you have likely not heard of this word, and yet, in my time, it was a scientific constant.

A zefluetic balance is when perfect harmony is achieved. It makes a noise that some sensitive souls can attune to. If spiritual or religious, one might call it the "song of angels" or "a choir of angels singing" in unison.

When vibrations line up for extended periods of time, a zefluetic balance is maintained. When differing chords are struck, there is strife.

If you watch your weather channel, you'll understand that when hot and cold weather collide, it creates a storm. In the United States, where Michelle resides, that's why there are often storms in the Midwest. The same can happen when a high frequency and a low vibe collide. Think of it like a storm in Kansas, with big hail and thunderstorms.

How do you stay out of the storm? By lining up with vibrational people, places, and experiences that make you hear the "hum" of the Universe. You'll know it when it happens. It is unmistakable.

If you find yourself in a storm, what do you do? Seek shelter. Retreat somewhere safe and heal yourself through the unique methods and tools only you know for your soul's highest and best. Then come out into the sunshine again, and sync up to your zefluetic tone.

When your world attains various tones of differing harmony, you will know peace. They don't all have to be the same to sound "right." The notes just have to work together.

## Lesson #105: Miracles Only Happen When You Believe Them

Miracles aren't miracles if you experience them every day.

You define your "miracles" as highly improbable events made of supernatural phenomenon that are welcome, surprising, and not explicable by scientific laws.

Once you completely believe in miracles, and therefore you see them occur more often—maybe even daily—they will become probable instead of improbable. They will become natural instead of supernatural. And, although still very welcome, they will not be surprising anymore.

Your "science" still may not be able to explain them, but scientists tend to look more at the visible than the invisible. As the invisible becomes visible, it becomes quantum physics, and scientists write about a bunch of guesses that may or may not become proven.

When you no longer need "proof," you will see more miracles. When you dwell in the miraculous, you will see more miracles. When you see more miracles, they won't be miracles anymore.

## Lesson #106: There is More That You Don't Know Than You Do Know

When you can accept that there is more you don't know than you do know, you can live in peace.

You may reject that notion, and that is purely up to you. When you stand in resistance, you will feel slighted and in pain. When you allow the thought to occur that maybe you don't know everything and that that is okay, you are in an open state for wisdom to occur.

Wisdom is not the same as knowledge. You accumulate knowledge like a computer stores information on its hard drive. Too much knowledge can crash your hard drive when ego takes center stage and thinks it knows all. You don't know all. How could you? You are still in a body.

Wisdom comes from transcendence of the body. You can do this, ironically, while still in the confines of dense matter. Accept that you know nothing, and you will know everything. It sounds like a conundrum, but we want you to sit with this notion and see how it makes you feel.

Accept that you know nothing, and you will know everything.

Repeat this throughout your day, and observe what shows up for you. Is it a sense of belonging? That's good. Does it make you angry? Let's explore that—why are you angry? What are you so angry about? Can you channel that anger into making the world a more peaceful place or are you adding to the suffering of the planet?

When you get to the space where we reside, you will see how silly and fruitless anger really is. We understand you have that in your vibration as it stands, but as you spiritually evolve, you will know less and less of it. For now, as it shows up, honor and respect it, and use it for the good of all. Channel it into power, like a nuclear power plant. Just don't let it explode.

If you don't like being told you know nothing, how does being told you know everything feel? Both are opinions. And yet, the Truth will resonate with you at a deeper level.

## Lesson #107: Cellular Direction and Division

When you are first born, your cells multiply and divide, multiply and divide, until the form and shape of a human can be ascertained.

In many incarnations, I worked as a doctor in various countries with differing medicinal backgrounds and ideas. And yet, it always returns to the same thing, doesn't it? Your cells multiply and divide, multiply and divide, until there is no more need for cellular growth and your soul is set free.

Have you accepted yet that your body is a microcosm of the macrocosm of the entire Universe? Have you realized and accepted as Truth that your individual soul is a microcosm of the macrocosm of Spirit? When this body and this lifetime story as you know it ends, you simply return to the greater part of You and are enveloped into Spirit. You may still individualize so that other souls might recognize you, and yet, you are all part of the greater whole.

Your body is, in effect, like a planet in your solar system. Eventually, planets explode—and so do stars.

When at its base form, your cells also can explode. Disease is like a big bang for your body, but just as the Universe as a whole does not change based on what matter and gases and light explode, your body's cellular explosion does not have an effect on your soul OR your spirit. Your soul, as part of Spirit, is like a great and still ocean. Even if there is an earthquake or tsunami below, it does not change the constitution of the entire ocean. It just may be a bit turbulent for a while.

Give your cells direction when they feel "turbulent." Your cells take direction from your mind's authority. Tell the healthy ones to heal and multiply, and allow the weak and diseased cells to slough off and be gone. Talk to your cells. Give them direction.

Try this for one week, and report the results. Do you feel healthier and more alive by talking to your cells? If you have been struggling with a physical condition of the body, has it gotten any better by this practice? If not, please continue on. If so, please continue on. Either way, it works eventually. If it doesn't? You have the option of receiving stem cells from other sources, which do not harm. Please explore them. Your bodies were created in order that your cells could multiply and divide. Do you need an injection of healthy cells? They are available everywhere, from the amniotic sacs of women giving birth through Cesarean section, to cord blood, even from fat. Why would you trash such life-giving health remedies? If your belief system counters such methods, please explore why, as we have done in other sections of this book.

Michelle received a stem cell injection to re-grow her digestive lining that was eroded due to celiac disease. There are zero side effects and only opportunities to re-grow and thrive! We experimented with stem cells hundreds of years ago, and yet, you have easier and less invasive methods to retrieve and harvest them than ever before. Please don't throw it all away.

## Lesson #108: Forgiveness

Building upon the last lesson, perhaps you don't feel as if you deserve greatness or that you do not already have greatness within you.

We have already pointed out to you in the last book that if you designed this life story—as well as the many, many others you have already lived out—there is no reason to forgive, as every single person you encounter is just playing out a role you assigned them in order for you to grow and learn lessons. That's it. They're doing you a favor!

And yet, we would like to take it a step further here.

Forgiveness is a daily act of shedding selves that no longer serve you or others.

If you accept that there are multiple dimensions in the beyond—where we reside—then please understand that you may release any "selves" that no longer work toward your highest and best.

For example, if you are having a day when it seems as if everything is going "wrong," and it feels as if everyone else is "against" you, perhaps you are living out a life that doesn't belong in the greater story of the highest version of You.

Kick it out of the game! Or at least "bench" that part of you. You did not come here to always get it wrong and to not have allies on your journey. Retreat, utilize some healing tools, perhaps reach out to another healer who vibes with you or even a little higher than you do, and get back on track.

It is possible. Everything is possible, remember? You have so many lifetimes going on right now, it's okay if you want to let go of a few. You're allowed.

## Lesson #109: Expanding into Everything

At this point in your development, you may feel on top of the world! As you rise and rise and rise and rise (times 10), you will feel fully alive and aware, full of joy and bliss and understanding!

And yet, there might still be those who use force to go after your brighter energy. Many healers and Light workers have been taught to deflect such negative energy through the use of "bubble" visualization or picturing their feet as tree roots going down into the earth. And those are all good practices.

Once you reach the epitome of your greatness, those who wish to be negative will not be anywhere near your "range" and won't be able to affect you at all! And yet, while you are on the way "up," you can play with the notion of becoming one with everything—including them—and letting it run through you like water.

This again builds on the last lessons. If you know your greatness, you will understand *you can handle this*. If fear arises, you are not ready. Do not "push" through the fear—that is only using force, and we recommend *never* using force. When you are in a relaxed, meditative state, perhaps see the entire earth enveloped in Light and Love, which we have already instructed. Now expand this brightness times 10!

As you know now, you are one with this same Light; allow it to encompass you as well, and now allow the biggest, highest part of You to become bigger and higher until it is bigger than your world. **Now merge with it.** Perhaps imagine swallowing your planet and allowing it to become one with you—flaws and all. You can digest this. You can allow for it all, for you have reached this place of Truth and understanding and clarity.

When you are done with this practice, please write down your feelings in your journal. Was there any unpleasantness involved? Did you feel uneasy swallowing the "bad" parts? Do you see now how your Light body—the greater part of You—is able to accept all those parts into itself and still expand?

## Lesson #110: Your Peace is Your Prosperity

Eudicine pointed out that your peace is your power. It is agreed, of course, by all of us. There is no balance of power amongst us, for there is nothing to take over, nothing to engage with—there is always, only, perfect harmony.

That is true for you as well, you see. When you understand that your inner peace creates the external peace present in your world, you will also realize that peace is your best and highest form of currency.

Peace is shared in the same way your currency is, yes? It is exchanged, not for services rendered or for products, but by virtue of you extolling your peace everywhere you go. If you were to live in a constant state of peace, you would attract everything to you at all times, as people can feel your peace and match it to the best of their ability (dependent upon the variation of your current vibrational offering).

As peace is spread, both internally and externally, there will be no need for other forms of currency, as peace begets more peace. When you are in a constant state of peace, you automatically know kindness. And kindness begets generosity. *Are you starting to comprehend how big this really is?*

When you are kind and generous, you will give out whatever you receive, and in this constant give and take, ebb and flow, you will find perfect union. There will be no more suffering from poverty or harsh conditions, from violence at the hands of another.

As long as you still inhabit a body, you will still experience pain, but as you rise, even that will lessen! Your suffering is still—always and ever—a reflection of how you view your pain.

As your perspective changes, so will your level of suffering and awareness of desire. There is nothing to desire when you know you have everything.

# THE BOOK OF LAVINIA

## LESSON #111: NO PROBLEMS

Deep within her vibration, Michelle summoned us through her unconscious question of why she still has "problems."

What are problems, really? You have no problems, ever. Your only "problem" is one of perception. In this moment, right here, right now, there *is* no problem. It is only your awareness of an alleged past and future that exist in space and time that create your obstacles and challenges.

If there is no time (and there's not—we've established it is but a man-made concept), what is left? *Financial problems?* Money is a man-made object and conceptual belief around energy. In Truth, you are always free. *Ill health?* Your body is now dense matter, but you can rise above pain with your focus and vibrate higher, or your body may need to be "repurposed," and your soul may need to return to Spirit. Either way is not a "problem." *Relationship problems?* Perhaps you are simply experiencing a change of frequency. Focus on yourself and the beauty ever present all around you, and the "other person" will either align with you or move on to learn their own lessons. Either way, you remain happy and lit up from within with joy.

What other problems are *yours*?

*War?* Not YOUR problem. As we have said countless times, once you've attained peace from within EACH of your souls, you will see it reflected in your world. You are not there yet. If you still fight against it, you will keep it going. That's the way it works.

*World hunger?* There are copious amounts of food sources and water on your planet as long as you learn to share. Once you learn to master manifestation and allow it to flow over like a fountain, you will each give to another who is hungry or without basic survival needs, which will also work to counteract violence acted out of desperation. If another is despairing, so are you. You are all connected. So don't *save* them, but *care* for them ... feed, clothe, and shelter one another, then allow them to have their own experiences beyond the basics.

I would like for you to write down any perceived problems you are creating at the moment. Ask yourself how they might be remedied or how you might choose to look at them differently. Be sure you are not speaking of past or future matters—by connecting with them, you are choosing to vibrate at that level of reality, which does not have to be. Be your highest and best Self, always.

## LESSON #112: INTENSE PRESENCE

When you find yourself mired in your past memories, you are bringing that energy into your Now.

Any feelings of guilt or shame are indicators that you are not being in present time. Acknowledge the memory that is causing the thoughts that are bringing the unpleasant feelings into your current experience, and then SHUT IT DOWN.

That's right. You heard us correctly. Just turn the switch to the "off" position, for it isn't happening at all in physical-time reality. Yes, it is happening in another dimension, and *your uneasy feelings are bringing it forward.*

The answer? Intense presence.

Let's break that down for you. *Intense* is an extreme force of concentration. It is fueled by inner strength. *Presence* is the state or the fact of existing.

And so, if you concentrate all your energies on your current state of existing, you will remain present in your Now, which is your highest form of be-ing.

This does not mean being in a state of "high alert," as if you are afraid of something happening to you. That is the opposite of what we mean here. It is more like being in a state of "welcoming," as in welcoming in whatever occurs, without your reaction. It is neutral, and yet it is being fully alive and aware. It is like being in the heightened state of initial romantic love, only all the time and in love with everything and everyone, as a form of total and complete acceptance.

That is Truth.

Start by claiming that you are here, now. Say it: "I am here, now." "I am here, I am here, I am here." Say it until you feel it—and when your thoughts stray, as they will—don't get mad, just bring them back into center by claiming your place, by affirming which dimension you are in, which will always be the highest and best one as long as you don't hold it back. Affirm that you are worthy and deserving of living your highest and best, right here. In *this* moment, for as long as it took you to read "THIS," you are at your highest and best. Claim it.

## LESSON #113: WALK AWAY FROM DRAMA

When you find yourself at the other end of blame and judgment, whether or not you believe you were the cause of it, walk away and work on healing yourself first.

This is what we are recommending to Michelle right now, as the higher she finds herself in frequency and vibration—and the longer she is able to maintain it—there are those who feel uncomfortable enough in her presence that they are actively attempting to drag her down.

In her situation, another family member keeps bringing up a past incident that is not remembered the same way for Michelle. She finds herself alternating between feelings of guilt and sadness and anger at not having any control over how others, especially those she loves, see her.

She was listening to a podcast and heard, "paralyzing guilt will not solve anything." That phrase leaped out at her because it matched her thoughts of "how do I get out of this?" She also heard to start thinking of her guilt as "selfish," for it gets in the way and blocks opportunities for her *and* them.

As this resonated with her, and because she does not like to view herself as "selfish," but as a knower of oneness and Truth, she decided to simply let it all go. She imagined letting go of a rope that was carrying something quite heavy, and she released the burden, because in Truth, this was not her lesson to learn. She was carrying the weight (again) of someone else's lesson for them—and as much as we might love them—that is not *unconditional* Love, for that is something else entirely. When you truly love another, you let them learn their own lessons, even if that means it is "self-destructive" or even if it means they don't share their journey with you for a while—or even for a lifetime.

When Michelle wrote that last line, we felt her heart "sink" a little, which means she is still learning the lesson of ultimately letting go. She will get there. You are all still learning, even our friend Michelle. If she could only see the BIG picture, from where we stand, she would know how light and airy it feels on the other side of letting go. That is true freedom, and it is indeed possible.

## Lesson #114: A State of Belonging

At the root of much of your suffering is a feeling of aloneness, of a lack of connection with humanity and others who understand you and where you are in life.

That is why you seek each other out.

Terrorists are not born in a vacuum. Most aren't all mentally ill, either. Many are highly intelligent and crave the same sort of connections you do. When they find empathy with a cause, they reach out—and because they feel more weak alone than in a group—they fall prey to the group belief system, even if it is one of violence.

If that same "terrorist," which just means inspiring fear in another, were to be accepted by all (would be embraced as a child into knowing that they, too, were part of all that is, that they were Divine in nature, and this lifetime was all just a giant "play," and they were one of the actors), perhaps they would not find resonance with a group that advocated violence and murder as solutions.

Group pressure and the need to belong contribute to terrorism. In fact, *you* contribute to the goals of terrorism every time you are fearful or angry at an attack, for you add to the collective unconscious feelings of terror and rage. *It is all energy, remember?*

Michelle was watching a television program about terrorism last night. (*Through the Wormhole*, narrated by Morgan Freeman). The show followed a group of evolutionary anthropologists who experimented about how to "unfreeze" minds over the Israeli-Palestinian conflict.

One researcher posed that you can change minds by simply agreeing with them. The group handed out flyers and posted billboards agreeing that a conflict was necessary, rather than pleading with them to make peace. It worked. Many started to question whether or not a conflict was indeed necessary.

We live in a positive-moving Universe—why wouldn't it be simpler to just agree with someone else? Arguing your point only proves to escalate a fight.

In war, many often *do* escalate their positions by seeing who can be the most ruthless—and all this results in is more fatalities for everyone!

Another researcher suggested an alternate way to peace is to "do nothing."

Complete disengagement results in the eventual "petering out" of the energy of the fight. The TV show used the example of playing a game of backgammon. If the person finds themselves playing the game without a partner, it's over.

The same is true of conflict. Don't feed it with fear and anger.

As the great, ascended master teacher Jesus said, "Turn the other cheek." We say, "Look away." Allow the fire to die down on its own.

Your greatest "weapon" is openness to new ideas.

## LESSON #115: PARENTING

I personally chose not to have children my last go-around in your lifecycles.

I'd had the experience of parenting many, many times, in various incarnations, and in the end, wanted to transition into teaching—which is what I am doing right now, but from a different plane of existence than I had originally intended.

We are all teachers in various forms, though, aren't we? Just as we are all students of life. It is by your example that others learn, for as we said in the last lesson, every one of you wants to belong. It is a part of the longing to be whole again, to be one with Spirit, which of course you already are, you just don't always remember …

As you "be-long"—as you long to be with one another's soul state—you gravitate in frequency toward those who vibe with you, as we've stated before. As you partner up with others who share your vibe (whether or not they *stay* there is immaterial at this point) you often procreate by the intention of your Love to multiply! Out of this intention, whether conscious or unconscious, you procreate. Look at that word you created to point to the multiplication of cellular life on your planet: pro-create.

And as you procreate, you often form an attachment to the child growing within you or within the body capsule of someone you love or who acts as a surrogate. With this attachment comes all sorts of expectations of how this growing person will turn out—whether exactly like you or in opposition to how you see yourself and your life story.

This attachment often continues into childhood as you share bonding experiences, and you keep them fed and clothed and out of harm's way as much as possible. Those who do not care for their children in such a way leave them to fend for themselves—often through a prior soul agreement to foster independence and self sufficiency—such as in Michelle's chosen childhood.

Others attach too much, and leave their children little wiggle room to grow and develop on their own.

We suggest a balanced approach, as in most things. Care for your young, feed them and clothe them and send them down the path of education and learning, and yet, stay out of their way! Love on them, just as you would anyone else, and love them enough to *watch* as they make their own mistakes and learn their own lessons.

This may be the hardest lesson of all. It is certainly something Michelle is going through currently, as we have discussed but choose not to dwell on. When Michelle dwells on the story of her child's alleged "abandonment" of her, it triggers the abandonment she felt as a child.

This was all planned, of course, pre-birth. It is part of why I am here, why I match the frequency of this particular group of spirits, to guide Michelle through this trying time and learn her soul's pre-birth lesson of freedom and independence from thought and judgment.

When she lets this go, it won't be her last lesson. Oh no, and we are laughing together at the thought Michelle just had that "this was it." It's never over. The suffering lessens, as you rise higher and higher in frequency and start seeing the "big picture" and living from that state of Truth in motion.

And yet, that Truth is always in **motion**. It is a moving "target" that you will never, ever reach! This is not being defeatist. Not in the least! It is part of the letting-go process, the surrendering to the **Now**, the allowing of the flow of ever-present **good** to move through you and *with* you that will get you to the radiant place where you lead by shining example.

So do you let go of your "goals"? Of course not. Only if you feel you must have them in a specific way to be "happy." We've said this before, but we'll reiterate: **Be happy now.**

Say it again. "Be happy now." Tell yourself this when you find your mind reaching hard into the future. That future is happening *now*. Tap into it.

You do not need things, people, or experiences to be happy. We are all gloriously happy all the time, and we do not have anything! We have, instead, EVERYTHING. You will realize this when you check out. And the irony is—when you see you do not need anything at all, that is when you will have everything.

What does this have to do with parenting?

Everything.

For when you *demonstrate* that you need for nothing, and you show by your glowing state of be-ing that you have everything, as you draw all things toward you in this lifetime (knowing that in the great BEYOND where we reside that that is the frequency you will all eventually achieve), you will inspire your offspring to do the same.

If not this lifetime, in the next, or the next … however long it takes for your children, as well as *any* soul you encounter and may not even physically birth, to truly "get it."

**They see you.** Your children may not tell you in words or even show you in actions that they see how you "play" in the world. And if you have been awful to them? Perhaps you had a prior soul agreement to act in such a way that they would learn by contrast from your negative example. Forgive yourself, for it is *all* planned pre-birth. We've said this before, but it is worth mentioning again—what is there to forgive if *you* planned it all out for the lessons it would teach you?

This lets you "off the hook," when you see where you stand from our perspective. You are all acting in accordance from your soul's greater plan for growth and expansion! Every one of you. You are all part of the "game" of life, just playing differing roles in a play, until you feel balanced enough to let go and float in bliss.

And so, looked at in this way, forgiving is not an *act*. It is more of a state of generosity and grace—for when you give, you are set free.

To undo any lower-vibing feelings such as shame and guilt and resentment, GIVE. Give generously and freely to one and all—not just your own kids! Give to the children of your planet, so that all may thrive. When you stay stuck in guilt and like emotions, you prevent the forward movement of the planet. You are tired and feel useless.

Get out of the guilt. It serves no one.

If your children no longer vibe with you as they age, let them live their own life stories and picture them bathed in loving Light. Affirm that they live their highest and best life, just as you affirm for one and all. See it, believe it. Picture a dandelion, if you must, and make a wish, and let it go. A "wish" is not "bad," as some might suggest. It is hopeful thinking. Make it stronger by *knowing* it is already so.

Do this for yourself, this visualization of living your highest and best Self, bathed in Light and Love as the highest expression of life, and you will no doubt do it for all—including your kids.

## Lesson #116: A Day at the Beach

Imagine yourself now, in this moment, at the beach.

It doesn't matter if you do not "like" the beach. Scroll through your memory banks until an image resonates with you that *feels* like freedom and wandering. It could be white sands and teal waters. It could be pebbles near a river or lake. It could even be a forest or a park in the middle of a big city center.

Imagine yourself there now. No worries, no cares, no thoughts, no opinions, no beliefs. Listen to the sounds around you. What are they? How does it smell? Is there a taste to the air? Heighten your senses now. Imagine a dial before you that you may turn up or turn down—now choose to turn up all your senses. What do you intuit? What messages are coming to you now?

How do you feel at the moment? Say, "Rise." Say it again and again until you feel the amplified state of being that feels good. Linger there. Listen to the sounds of the "beach"—beach yourself there for a while. Pause. Renew.

Know that you can go here at any time.

## Lesson #117: When Nothing Matters

When no-thing matters, everything comes into matter.

This may seem like some sort of Zen proverb, and perhaps contradictory in nature, but sit with it for some time in meditation and see what pops up for you in relation to this statement.

Practice saying to yourself today, "Nothing matters."

You can say it in differing ways, if you wish.

"It doesn't matter."

"It just doesn't matter."

As long as you don't feel in resistance to what shows up for you, you can state emphatically that nothing matters, without your support and agreement.

Now, having said that and put it into effect, please document what occurs when you practice being in a state of "nothing matters."

Did "things" pop up in your experience? If not, please do this for more than a day …

Again, you brought yourself into matter by your intention to have a dense life, where you could mold and shape new experiences and adventures just by focusing thought. With your support and agreement, you may *decide* to bring something forth into your experience.

Something new that Michelle is bringing forth into matter: an opportunity to teach yoga on the beach for a week at a five-star resort in Cancun, Mexico. This excites Michelle, for as she writes, her heart beats loudly.

Michelle was in an "empty" state of meditation where she visualized white sand beaches and tropical drinks and conjured the feelings and energy of wandering and freedom.

When she returned to her desk, she received an email from a company she had contracted with years ago. Because it resonated with her, she scrolled through the opportunities and found the one in Cancun that felt exactly like the vision she had in meditation!

She brought forth this experience into matter, because she reached the frequency of "it doesn't matter."

Seems like a paradox, but it's not. Try it out.

## Lesson #118: Embrace and Unplug

You understand, now, that you have many parallel lives ongoing at the very same time—sort of like a million television sets on differing channels but all in the same room.

In order to be your highest and best Self at any given time, you can play with the notion of all of your other "selves" hugging and embracing you until you feel loved and deserving of this best life. Imagine it now. Picture all of your selves loving on you, like a big pile of puppies.

In the same way, you may choose to disengage from your more destructive "selves" that no longer serve you. Simply allow those "characters" to step forward and reveal themselves to you in meditation, and picture yourself "unplugging" from their energy source. Really do it—envision the plug and the cord and the outlet, all disengaging from this particular negative version of yourself.

In this way, you may ride your soul of attachments to alternate dimensional realities before you leave this platform of life.

## Lesson #119: Survivor

So often when you go exploring your past lifetimes and their various stories and lessons and traumas, you go into victim mode, which serves zero purpose.

Remember, please, that those lifetimes are going on right *now*. We keep repeating that because we don't feel as if it's sunk in yet, and we are reaching the end of this particular book.

Affirming your best and brightest Self means you *are* a survivor. Let this sink in: your soul is a survivor! Your soul has survived some of the worst things imaginable, and yet, it's still here, shiny and new as if it had never gone through anything at all.

Because, in Truth, it hasn't. Your personality in each moment has told a story—countless stories, in fact. And yet, you know the Truth by how it resonates in your body first (in Michelle's body it often reflects as goose bumps) and then how it feels deep in your soul.

How does it feel to know your soul is *surviving*?! Even that term is a bit defeating, and so, we'd like to use the word "thriving," because that's closer to it, wouldn't you say?

When your life story seems a challenge, please affirm that your soul thrives—always and in every way possible. Stop the current drama in your head, and turn it around by saying:

"My soul thrives."

How does THAT feel?

## Lesson #120: Everything Serves to Heal

Your entire holographic reality that *you* created out of nothing is here to serve you by healing you.

In Truth, you are already healed. You know that by now, as we are coming upon the end of this particular book. There will be more, indeed. But for now, please know that you are already healed, whole, complete—exactly how you are.

By now, we sincerely see you thriving! That is our hope and desire for you as we come through Michelle to teach. There is no alternative function other than this: to move humanity forward by pointing you all toward what you already know at your core.

You know you are One. You know you are a microcosmic representation of the macrocosm of the entire Universe! You understand now that the Universe is not a person, but a vibrational, forward-moving force that you simply need to match frequencies with in order to have and hold all that you desire while still inhabiting a dense body.

You realize that as you become a master manifestor, and as you enjoy all the things and experiences you can possibly experience on your planet, you are learning to give it away and watch it return ten-fold. Is that happening for you yet? Are you giving what you receive?

You feel good more often than you feel bad now, yes? If not, please reread the first book and this one in their entirety until you do. You are supposed to live a life of joy and freedom! That was and always is your eternal mission. If it's too much in this elementary existence, please know that there is so much <u>beyond</u> your current dimensional understanding. Just know this: that's all you have to do. And when you leave this particular body behind, you will have a new awareness that more exists.

Beyond exists. There is indeed a place beyond suffering where you will know only faith. For now, practice faith and trust daily, know you are made up of Love and only Love, and cherish the good feelings that come from your earthly existence. Let go of the made-up stories of past, present, and future—they don't truly exist or matter. All that is of consequence is your current now. Take the pressure off of yourself by living from this state of presence.

When you live from this higher state of Truth, you will continue gathering and attracting and magnetizing the way *we* do, here in the dimensions beyond time and space. Your master teacher Albert Einstein figured out that time moves differently for different people (special vs. general relativity), corresponding to their relative speed. Time and space are fluid, and so are you. So are we.

And so, we leave you with this: Be fluid and free. Don't inhibit yourself by dwelling on whatever alleged "blocks" you think you are creating. Create a more open, loving, trusting acceptance with your life, and your life will bring you more.

Until next time, we are—The Power of 10.

# ABOUT THE AUTHOR

Michelle Paisley Reed is a world-renowned author, inspirational speaker, and spirit channel. She's written four screenplays and five books (and counting), including the first two in this series, *Manifesting Miracles and Money: How to Achieve Peace, Purpose, and Plenty Without Getting in Your Own Way*, and *Peace is Power: A Course in Shifting Reality Through Science and Spirituality*. Other books by

Michelle include: *Yoga for a Broken Heart, All in Her Head,* and *All Over It.*

She has authored an oracle card app called "All in One" through Indiegoes.com. A new reality TV show, "Don't Change The Channel," is currently in development. Michelle is a former news journalist and lives with her husband, 10 spirit guides, a dog, and two cats in Northern California.

## CONNECT WITH MICHELLE AND THE POWER OF 10

Website: www.WeArethePowerOf10.com

Facebook: www.facebook.com/WeArethePowerOf10

Instagram: www.instagram.com/wearethepowerof10

Twitter: www.twitter.com/wearepowerof10

Pinterest: www.pinterest.com/powerof10

Join The Power of 10 "High Vibe Tribe" in our private Facebook Group:

*www.facebook.com/groups/ PowerOf10HighVibeTribe*

# OTHER BOOKS BY
# MICHELLE PAISLEY REED

Manifesting Miracles and Money: How to Achieve Peace, Purpose, and Plenty Without Getting in Your Own Way (http://a.co/ifzZtwk)

Yoga for a Broken Heart: A Spiritual Guide to Healing from Break-up, Loss, Death or Divorce (http://a.co/2oqj8Mx)

All in Her Head (http://a.co/1xUMjzh)

All Over It (http://a.co/hxcejya)

# Book Discounts
## and Special Deals

Sign up for free to get discounts and special deals on our best selling books at

www.tckpublishing.com/bookdeals

www.ingramcontent.com/pod-product-compliance
Lightning Source LLC
Chambersburg PA
CBHW070053080526
44586CB00013B/1034